Monologues from Shakespeare's First Folio for Older Men: *The Histories*

The Applause Shakespeare Monologue Series

Other Shakespeare Titles From Applause

Once More unto the Speech Dear Friends
Volume One: The Comedies
Compiled and Edited with Commentary by Neil Freeman

Once More unto the Speech Dear Friends
Volume Two: The Histories
Compiled and Edited with Commentary by Neil Freeman

Once More unto the Speech Dear Friends
Volume Three: The Tragedies
Compiled and Edited with Commentary by Neil Freeman

The Applause First Folio in Modern Type
Prepared and Annotated by Neil Freeman

The Folio Texts
Prepared and Annotated by Neil Freeman, Each of the 36 plays of the
Applause First Folio in Modern Type individually bound

The Applause Shakespeare Library
Plays of Shakespeare Edited for Performance

Soliloquy: The Shakespeare Monologues

Monologues from Shakespeare's First Folio for Older Men:
The Histories

Compilation and Commentary by
Neil Freeman

Edited by
Paul Sugarman

APPLAUSE
THEATRE & CINEMA BOOKS
Guilford, Connecticut

APPLAUSE
THEATRE & CINEMA BOOKS

An imprint of Globe Pequot, the trade division of
The Rowman & Littlefield Publishing Group, Inc.
4501 Forbes Blvd., Ste. 200
Lanham, MD 20706
www.rowman.com

Distributed by NATIONAL BOOK NETWORK

Library of Congress Cataloging-in-Publication Data available

Library of Congress Control Number: 2021944365

ISBN 978-1-4930-5696-5 (paperback)
ISBN 978-1-4930-5697-2 (ebook)

Dedication

Although Neil Freeman passed to that "undiscovered country" in 2015, his work continues to lead students and actors to a deeper understanding of Shakespeare's plays. With the exception of Shakespeare's words (and my humble foreword), the entirety of the material within these pages is Neil's. May these editions serve as a lasting legacy to a life of dedicated scholarship, and a great passion for Shakespeare.

Contents

FOREWORD

Paul Sugarman

Monologues from Shakespeare's First Folio presents the work of Neil Freeman, longtime champion of Shakespeare's First Folio, whose groundbreaking explorations into how first printings offered insights to the text in rehearsals, stage and in the classroom. This work continued with *Once More Unto the Speech Dear Friends: Monologues from Shakespeare's First Folio with Modern Text Versions for Comparison* where Neil collected over 900 monologues divided between the Comedy, History and Tragedy Published by Applause in three masterful volumes which present the original First Folio text side by side with the modern, edited version of the text. These volumes provide a massive amount of material and information. However both the literary scope, and the literal size of these volumes can be intimidating and overwhelming. This series' intent is to make the work more accessible by taking material from the encyclopediac original volumes and presenting it in an accessible workbook format.

To better focus the work for actors and students the texts are contrasted side by side with introductory notes before and commentary after to aid the exploration of the text. By comparing modern and First Folio printings, Neil points the way to gain new insights into Shakespeare's text. Editors over the centuries have "corrected" and updated the texts to make them "accessible," or "grammatically correct." In doing so they have lost vital clues and information that Shakespeare placed there for his actors. With the texts side by side, you can see where and why editors have made changes and what may have been lost in translation.

In addition to being divided into Histories, Comedies, and Tragedies, the original series further breaks down speeches by the character's designated gender, also indicating speeches appropriate for any gender. Drawing from this example, this series breaks down each original volume into four workbooks: speeches for Women of all ages, Younger Men, Older Men and Any Gender. Gender is naturally fluid for Shakespeare's characters since during his time, ALL of the characters were portrayed by males. Contemporary productions of Shakespeare commonly switch character genders (Prospero has become Prospera), in addition to presenting single gender, reverse gender and gender non-specific productions. There are certainly characters and speeches where the gender is immaterial, hence the inclusion of a volume of speeches for Any Gender. This was something that Neil had indicated in the original volumes; we are merely following his example.

The monologues in the book are arranged by play in approximate order of composition, so you get his earliest plays first and can observe how his rhetorical art developed over time. The speeches are then arranged by their order in the play.

Once More Unto the Speech Dear Friends was a culmination of Neil's dedicated efforts to make the First Folio more accessible and available to readers and to illuminate for actors the many clues within the Folio text, as originally published. The material in this book is drawn from that work and retains Neil's British spelling of words (i.e. capitalisation) and his extensive commentary on each speech. Neil went on to continue this work as a master teacher of Shakespeare with another series of Shakespeare editions, his 'rhythm texts' and the ebook that he published on Apple Books, *The Shakespeare Variations.*

Neil published on his own First Folio editions of the plays in modern type which were the basis the Folio Texts series published by Applause of all 36 plays in the First Folio. These individual editions all have extensive notes on the changes that modern editions had made. This material was then combined to create a complete reproduction of the First Folio in modern type, *The Applause First Folio of Shakespeare in Modern Type.* These editions make the First Folio more accessible than ever before. The examples in this book demonstrate how the clues from the First Folio will give insights to understanding and performing these speeches and why it is a worthwhile endeavour to discover the riches in the First Folio.

PREFACE AND BRIEF BACKGROUND TO THE FIRST FOLIO

WHY ANOTHER SERIES OF SOLILOQUY BOOKS?

There has been an enormous change in theatre organisation recent in the last twenty years. While the major large-scale companies have continued to flourish, many small theatre companies have come into being, leading to

- much doubling
- cross gender casting, with many one time male roles now being played legitimately by/as women in updated time-period productions
- young actors being asked to play leading roles at far earlier points in their careers

All this has meant actors should be able to demonstrate enormous flexibility rather than one limited range/style. In turn, this has meant

- a change in audition expectations
- actors are often expected to show more range than ever before
- often several shorter audition speeches are asked for instead of one or two longer ones
- sometimes the initial auditions are conducted in a shorter amount of time

Thus, to stay at the top of the game, the actor needs more knowledge of what makes the play tick, especially since

- early plays demand a different style from the later ones
- the four genres (comedy, history, tragedy, and the peculiar romances) all have different acting/textual requirements
- parts originally written for the older, more experienced actors again require a different approach from those written for the younger

ones, as the young roles, especially the female ones, were played by young actors extraordinarily skilled in the arts of rhetoric

There's now much more knowledge of how the original quarto and folio texts can add to the rehearsal exploration/acting and directing process as well as to the final performance.

Each speech is made up of four parts

- a background to the speech, placing it in the context of the play, and offering line length and an approximate timing to help you choose what might be right for any auditioning occasion
- a modern text version of the speech, with the sentence structure clearly delineated side by side with
- a folio version of the speech, where modern texts changes to the capitalization, spelling and sentence structure can be plainly seen
- a commentary explaining the differences between the two texts, and in what way the original setting can offer you more information to explore

Thus if they wish, **beginners** can explore just the background and the modern text version of the speech.

An actor experienced in exploring the Folio can make use of the background and the Folio version of the speech

And those wanting to know as many details as possible and how they could help define the deft stepping stones of the arc of the speech can use all four elements on the page.

The First Folio

(FOR LIST OF CURRENT REPRODUCTIONS SEE BIBLIOGRAPHY

The end of 1623 saw the publication of the justifiably famed First Folio (F1). The single volume, published in a run of approximately 1,000 copies at the princely sum of one pound (a tremendous risk, considering that a single play would sell at no more than six pence, one fortieth of F1's price, and that the annual salary of a schoolmaster was only ten pounds), contained thirty-six plays.

The manuscripts from which each F1 play would be printed came from a variety of sources. Some had already been printed. Some came from the playhouse complete with production details. Some had no theatrical input at all, but were handsomely copied out and easy to read. Some were supposedly very messy, complete with first draft scribbles and crossings out. Yet, as Charlton Hinman, the revered dean of First Folio studies describes F1 in the Introduction to the Norton Facsimile:

> It is of inestimable value for what it is, for what it contains. For here are preserved the masterworks of the man universally recognized as our greatest writer; and preserved, as Ben Jonson realized at the time of the original publication, not for an age but for all time.

WHAT DOES F1 REPRESENT?

- texts prepared for actors who rehearsed three days for a new play and one day for one already in the repertoire
- written in a style (rhetoric incorporating debate) so different from ours (grammatical) that many modern alterations based on grammar (or poetry) have done remarkable harm to the rhetorical/debate quality of the original text and thus to interpretations of characters at key moments of stress.
- written for an acting company the core of which steadily grew older, and whose skills and interests changed markedly over twenty years as well as for an audience whose make-up and interests likewise changed as the company grew more experienced

The whole is based upon supposedly the best documents available at the time, collected by men closest to Shakespeare throughout his career, and brought to a single printing house whose errors are now widely understood - far more than those of some of the printing houses that produced the original quartos.

TEXTUAL SOURCES FOR THE AUDITION SPEECHES
Individual modern editions consulted in the preparation of the Modern Text version of the speeches are listed in the Bibliography under the separate headings 'The Complete Works in Compendium Format' and ' The Complete Works in Separate Individual Volumes.' Most of the modern versions of the speeches are a compilation of several of these texts. However, all modern act, scene and/or line numbers refer the reader to The Riverside Shakespeare, in my opinion still the best of the complete works despite the excellent compendiums that have been published since.

The First Folio versions of the speeches are taken from a variety of already published sources, including not only all the texts listed in the 'Photostatted Reproductions in Compendium Format' section of the Bibliography, but also earlier, individually printed volumes, such as the twentieth century editions published under the collective title *The Facsimiles of Plays from The First Folio of Shakespeare* by Faber & Gwyer, and the nineteenth century editions published on behalf of The New Shakespeare Society.

INTRODUCTION

So, congratulations , you've got an audition, and for a Shakespeare play no less.

You've done all your homework, including, hopefully , reading the whole play to see the full range and development of the character.

You've got an idea of the character, the situation in which you/it finds itself (the given circumstance s); what your/its needs are (objectives/intentions); and what you intend to do about them (action /tactics).

You've looked up all the unusual words in a good dictionary or glossary; you've turned to a well edited modern edition to find out what some of the more obscure references mean.

And those of you who understand metre and rhythm have worked on the poetic values of the speech, and you are word perfect . . .

. . . and yet it's still not working properly and/or you feel there's more to be gleaned from the text , but you're not sure what that something is or how to go about getting at it; in other words, all is not quite right, yet.

THE KEY QUESTION

What text have you been working with - a good modern text or an 'original' text, that is a copy of one of the first printings of the play?

If it's a modern text, no matter how well edited (and there are some splendid single copy editions available, see the Bibliography for further details), despite all the learned information offered, it's not surprising you feel somewhat at a loss, for there is a huge difference between the original printings (the First Folio, and the individual quartos, see

Appendix 1 for further details) and any text prepared after 1700 right up to the most modern of editions. All the post 1700 texts have been tidied-up for the modern reader to ingest silently, revamped according to the rules of correct grammar, syntax and poetry. However the 'originals' were prepared for actors speaking aloud playing characters often in a great deal of emotional and/or intellectual stress, and were set down on paper according to the very flexible rules of rhetoric and a seemingly very cavalier attitude towards the rules of grammar, and syntax, and spelling, and capitalisation, and even poetry.

Unfortunately, because of the grammatical and syntactical standardisation in place by the early 1700's, many of the quirks and oddities of the origin also have been dismissed as 'accidental' - usually as compositor error either in deciphering the original manuscript, falling prey to their own particular idosyncracies, or not having calculated correctly the amount of space needed to set the text. Modern texts dismiss the possibility that these very quirks and oddities may be by Shakespeare, hearing his characters in as much difficulty as poor Peter Quince is in *A Midsummer Night's Dream* (when he, as the Prologue, terrified and struck down by stage fright, makes a huge grammatical hash in introducing his play 'Pyramus and Thisbe' before the aristocracy, whose acceptance or otherwise, can make or break him)

> If we offend, it is with our good will.
> That you should think, we come not to offend,
> But with good will.
>   To show our simple skill,
> That is the true beginning of our end .
> Consider then, we come but in despite.
> We do not come, as minding to content you ,
> Our true intent is.
>   All for your delight
> We are not here.
>   That you should here repent you,

The Actors are at hand; and by their show,
You shall know all, that you are like to know.

(A Midsummer Night's Dream)

In many other cases in the complete works what was originally printed is equally 'peculiar,' but, unlike Peter Quince , these peculiarities are usually regularised by most modern texts.

However, this series of volumes is based on the belief - as the following will show - that most of these 'peculiarities' resulted from Shakespeare setting down for his actors the stresses, trials, and tribulations the characters are experiencing as they think and speak, and thus are theatrical gold-dust for the actor, director, scholar, teacher, and general reader alike.

THE FIRST ESSENTIAL DIFFERENCE BETWEEN THE TWO TEXTS

THINKING

A **modern** text can show

- the story line
- your character's conflict with the world at large
- your character's conflict with certain individuals within that world

but because of the very way an 'original' text was set, it can show you all this plus one key extra, the very thing that makes big speeches what they are

- the conflict within the character

WHY?

Any good playwright writes about characters in stressful situations who are often in a state of conflict not only with the world around them and the people in that world, but also within themselves. And you probably know from personal experience that when these conflicts occur people do not necessarily utter the most perfect of grammatical/poetic/ syntactic statements, phrases, or sentences. Joy and delight, pain and sorrow often come sweeping through in the way things are said, in the incoherence of the phrases, the running together of normally disassociated ideas, and even in the sounds of the words themselves.

The tremendous advantage of the period in which Shakespeare was setting his plays down on paper and how they first appeared in print was that when characters were rational and in control of self and situation, their phrasing and sentences (and poetic structure) would appear to be quite normal even to a modern eye - but when things were going wrong, so sentences and phrasing (and poetic structure) would become highly erratic. But the Quince type eccentricities are rarely allowed to stand. Sadly, in tidying , most modern texts usually make the text far too clean, thus setting rationality when none originally existed.

THE SECOND ESSENTIAL DIFFERENCE BETWEEN THE TWO TEXTS
SPEAKING, ARGUING, DEBATING

Having discovered what and how you/your character is thinking is only the first stage of the work - you/it then have to speak aloud, in a society that absolutely loved to speak - and not only speak ideas (content) but to speak entertainingly so as to keep listeners enthralled (and this was especially so when you have little content to offer and have to mask it somehow - think of today 's television adverts and political spin doctors as a parallel and you get the picture). Indeed one of the Elizabethan 'how to win an argument' books was very precise about this - George Puttenham, *The Art of English Poesie* (1589).

A: ELIZABETHAN SCHOOLING

All educated classes could debate/argue at the drop of a hat, for both boys (in 'petty-schools') and girls (by books and tutors) were trained in what was known overall as the art of rhetoric, which itself was split into three parts

- first, how to distinguish the real from false appearances/outward show (think of the three caskets in *The Merchant of Venice* where the language on the gold and silver caskets enticingly, and deceptively, seems to offer hopes of great personal rewards that are dashed when the language is carefully explored, whereas once the apparent threat on the lead casket is carefully analysed the reward therein is the greatest that could be hoped for)

- second, how to frame your argument on one of 'three great grounds'; honour/morality; justice/legality; and, when all else fails, expedience/practicality.

- third, how to order and phrase your argument so winsomely that your audience will vote for you no matter how good the opposition - and there were well over two hundred rules and variations by which winning could be achieved, all of which had to be assimilated before a child's education was considered over and done with.

B: THINKING ON YOUR FEET: I.E. THE QUICK, DEFT , RAPID MODIFICATION OF EACH TINY THOUGHT

The Elizabethan/therefore your character/therefore you were also trained to explore and modify your thoughts as you spoke - never would you see a sentence in its entirety and have it perfectly worked out in your mind before you spoke (unless it was a deliberately written, formal public declaration, as with the Officer of the Court in The Winter' s Tale, reading the charges against Hermione). Thus after uttering your very first phrase, you might expand it, or modify it, deny it, change it, and so on throughout the whole sentence and speech.

From the poet Samuel Coleridge Taylor there is a wonderful description of how Shakespeare puts thoughts together like "a serpent twisting and untwisting in its own strength," that is, with one thought springing out of the one previous. Treat each new phrase as a fresh unravelling of the serpent's coil. What is discovered (and therefore said) is only revealed as the old coil/phrase disappears revealing a new coil in its place. The new coil is the new thought. The old coil moves/disappears because the previous phrase is finished with as soon as it is spoken.

C: MODERN APPLICATION

It is very rarely we speak dispassionately in our 'real' lives, after all thoughts give rise to feelings, feelings give rise to thoughts, and we usually speak both together - unless

1/ we're trying very hard for some reason to control ourselves and not give ourselves away

2/ or the volcano of emotions within us is so strong that we cannot control ourselves, and feelings swamp thoughts

3/ and sometimes whether deliberately or unconsciously we colour words according to our feelings; the humanity behind the words so revealed is instantly understandable.

D: HOW THE ORIGINAL TEXTS NATURALLY ENHANCE/ UNDERSCORE THIS CONTROL OR RELEASE

The amazing thing about the way all Elizabethan/early Jacobean texts were first set down (the term used to describe the printed words on the page being 'orthography'), is that it was flexible, it allowed for such variations to be automatically set down without fear of grammatical repercussion.

So if Shakespeare heard Juliet's nurse working hard to try to convince Juliet that the Prince's nephew Juliet is being forced to (bigamously) marry, instead of setting the everyday normal

'O he's a lovely gentleman'

which the modern texts HAVE to set, the first printings were permitted to set

'O hee's a Lovely Gentleman'

suggesting that something might be going on inside the Nurse that causes her to release such excessive extra energy.

E: BE CAREFUL

This needs to be stressed very carefully: the orthography doesn't dictate to you/force you to accept exactly what it means. The orthography simply suggests you might want to explore this moment further or more deeply.

In other words, simply because of the flexibility with which the Elizabethans/Shakespeare could set down on paper what they heard in their minds or wanted their listeners to hear, in addition to all the modern acting necessities of character - situation, objective, intention, action, and tactics the original Shakespeare texts offer pointers to where feelings (either emotional or intellectual, or when combined together as passion, both) are also evident.

SUMMARY

BASIC APPROACH TO THE SPEECHES SHOWN BELOW

(after reading the 'background')

1/ first use the modem version shown in the first column: by doing so you can discover
- the basic plot line of what's happening to the character, and
- the first set of conflicts/obstacles impinging on the character as a result of the situation or actions of other characters
- the supposed grammatical and poetical correctnesses of the speech

2/ then you can explore
- any acting techniques you'd apply to any modem soliloquy, including establishing for the character
- the given circumstances of the scene
- their outward state of being (who they are sociologically, etc.)
- their intentions and objectives
- the resultant action and tactics they decide to pursue

3/ when this is complete, turn to the First Folio version of the text, shown on the facing page: this will help you discover and explore
- the precise thinking and debating process so essential to an understanding of any Shakespeare text
- the moments when the text is NOT grammatically or poetically as correct as the modern texts would have you believe, which will in tum help you recognise
- the moments of conflict and struggle stemming from within the character itself
- the sense of fun and enjoyment the Shakespeare language nearly always offers you no matter how dire the situation

4/ should you wish to further explore even more the differences between the two texts, the commentary that follows discusses how the First Folio has been changed, and what those alterations might mean for the human arc of the speech

NOTES ON HOW THESE SPEECHES ARE SET UP

For each of the speeches the first page will include the Background on the speech and other information including number of lines, approximate timing and who is addressed. Then will follow a spread which shows the modern text version on the left and the First Folio version on the right, followed by a page of Commentary.

PROBABLE TIMING: (shown on the Background page before the speeches begin, set below the number of lines) 0.45 = a forty-five second speech

SYMBOLS & ABBREVIATIONS IN THE COMMENTARY AND TEXT

F: the First Folio

mt.: modern texts

F # followed by a number: the number of the sentence under discussion in the First Folio version of the speech, thus F #7 would refer to the seventh sentence

mt. # followed by a numb er: the number of the sentence under discussion in the modern text version of the speech, thus mt. #5 would refer to the fifth sentence

 # /#, (e.g. 3/7): the first number refers to the number of capital letters in the passage under discussion; the second refers to the number of long spellings therein

within a quotation from the speech: / indicates where one verse line ends and a fresh one starts

[ ] : set around words in both texts when Fl sets one word , mt another

{ } : some minor alteration has been made, in a speech built up, where, a word or phrase will be changed, added, or removed

{†} : this symbol shows where a sizeable part of the text is omitted

TERMS FOUND IN THE COMMENTARY
OVERALL

1/ **orthography**: the capitalization, spellings, punctuation of the First Folio
SIGNS OF IMPORTANT DISCOVERIES/ARGUMENTS WITHIN A FIRST FOLIO SPEECH

2/ **major punctuation**: colons and semicolons: since the Shakespeare texts are based so much on the art of debate and argument, the importance of F1 's major punctuation must not be underestimated, for both the semicolon (;) and colon (:) mark a moment of importance for the character, either for itself, as a moment of discovery or revelation, or as a key point in a discussion, argument or debate that it wishes to impress upon other characters onstage

as a rule of thumb:

a/ the more frequent colon (:) suggests that whatever the power of the point discovered or argued, the character is not side-tracked and can continue with the argument - as such, the colon can be regarded as a **logical** connection

b/ the far less frequent semicolon (;) suggests that because of the power inherent in the point discovered or argued, the character is side-tracked and momentarily loses the argument and falls back into itself or can only continue the argument with great difficulty - as such, the semicolon should be regarded as an **emotional** connection

3/ **surround phrases**: phrase(s) surrounded by major punctuation, or a combination of major punctuation and the end or beginning of a sentence: thus these phrases seem to be of especial importance for both character and speech, well worth exploring as key to the argument made and /or emotions released

DIALOGUE NOT FOUND IN THE FIRST FOLIO

∞ set where modern texts add dialogue from a quarto text which has not been included in Fl

A LOOSE RULE OF THUMB TO THE THINKING PROCESS OF A FIRST FOLIO CHARACTER

1/ mental discipline/**intellect**: a section where capitals dominate suggests that the intellectual reason ing behind what is being spoken or discovered is of more concern than the personal response beneath it

2/ feelings/**emotions**: a section where long spellings dominate suggests that the personal response to what is being spoken or discovered is of more concern than the intellectual reasoning behind it

3/ **passion**: a section where both long spellings and capitals are present in almost equal proportions suggests that both mind and emotion/feelings are inseparable, and thus the character is speaking passionately

SIGNS OF LESS THAN GRAMMATICAL THINKING WITHIN A FIRST FOLIO SPEECH

1/ **onrush**: sometimes thoughts are coming so fast that several topics are joined together as one long sentence suggesting that the F character's mind is working very quickly, or that his/her emotional state is causing some concern: most mod ern texts split such a sentence into several grammatically correct parts (the opening speech of *As You Like It* is a fine example, where F's long 18 line opening sentence is split into six): while the modern texts' resetting may be syntactically correct, the F moment is nowhere near as calm as the revisions suggest

2/ **fast-link**: sometimes F shows thoughts moving so quickly for a character that the connecting punctuation between disparate topics is merely a comma, suggesting that there is virtually no pause in springing from one idea to the next: unfortunately most modern texts rarely allow this to stand, instead replacing the obviously disturbed comma with a grammatical period, once more creating calm that it seems the original texts never intended to show

FIRST FOLIO SIGNS OF WHEN VERBAL GAME PLAYING HAS TO STOP

1/ **non-embellished:** a section with neither capitals nor long spellings suggests that what is being discovered or spoken is so important to the character that there is no time to guss it up with vocal or mental excesses: an unusual moment of self-control

2/ **short sentence:** coming out of a society where debate was second nature, man y of Shakespeare's characters speak in long sentences in which ideas are stated, explored, redefined and summarized all before moving onto the next idea in the argument, discovery or debate: the longer sentence is the sign of a rhetorically trained mind used to public speaking (oratory), but at times an idea or discovery is so startling or inevitable that length is either unnecessary or impossible to maintain : hence the occasional very important short sentence suggests that there is no time for the niceties of oratorical adornment with which to sugar the pill - verbal games are at an end and now the basic core of the issue must be faced

3/ **monosyllabic:** with English being composed of two strands, the polysyllabic (stemming from French, Italian, Latin and Greek), and the monosyllabic (from the Anglo-Saxon), each strand has two distinct functions: the polysyllabic words are often used when there is time for fanciful elaboration and rich description (which could be described as 'excessive rhetoric') while the monosyllabic occur when, literally, there is no other way of putting a basic question or comment - Juliet's "Do you love me? I know thou wilt say aye" is a classic example of both monosyllables and non-embellishment: with monosyllables, only the naked truth is being spoken, nothing is hidden

Monologues from Shakespeare's First Folio for Older Men: *The Histories*

The First Part of Henry the Sixt

Gloster

Presumptuous Priest, this place commands my patience,
3.1.8–26

Background: in the struggle to become the power behind Henry VI, the current holder of the English throne, Henry's politically oriented uncle Humfrey, Duke of Gloster, and his great-uncle the churchman Henry Beaufort, Bishop of Winchester, are at each other's throats, as are their respective supporters. Here, in the open court, Gloster publicly justifies his hitherto written (pamphlet) attacks on the Bishop.

Style: one on one for the benefit of a larger group

Where: the English Court

To Whom: Winchester, in front of Henry VI, Exeter, Warwicke, Somerset, Suffolk, and Yorke

# of Lines: 19

Probable Timing: 1.00 minutes

Take Note: While the sentence structure of the two texts almost matches, the F orthography highlights where Gloster allows his feelings to get the better of him instead of sticking to the task of shaming his enemy in public: though a debate is expected, and reinforced by most modern texts, F reveals anything but.

Gloster

1 Presumptuous priest, this place commands my
                                        patience,
   Or thou shouldst find thou hast dishonor'd me .

2 Think not, although in writing I preferr'd
   The manner of thy vile outrageous crimes,
   That therefore I have forg'd, or am not able
   Verbatim to rehearse [my method pen'd] .

3 No, prelate, such is thy audacious wickedness,
   Thy lewd, pestiferous, and dissentious pranks,
   As very infants prattle of thy pride .

4 Thou art a most pernicious usurer,
   Froward by nature, enemy to peace,
   Lascivious, wanton, more [than] well beseems
   A man of thy profession, and degree ;
   And for thy treachery, what's more manifest ?
   In that thou laidst a trap to take my life,
   As well at London Bridge as at the Tower .

5 Beside, I fear me, if thy thoughts were sifted,

Gloster

1   Presumptuous Priest, this place commands my
patience,
     Or thou should'st finde thou hast dis-honor'd me .

2   Thinke not, although in Writing I preferr'd
     The manner of thy vile outrageous Crymes,
     That therefore I have forg'd, or am not able
     Verbatim to rehearse [the Methode of my Penne] .

3   No Prelate, such is thy audacious wickednesse,
     Thy lewd, pestiferous, and dissentious prancks,
     As very Infants prattle of thy pride .

4   Thou art a most pernitious Usurer,
     Froward by nature, Enemie to Peace,
     Lascivious, wanton, more [then] well beseemes
     A man of thy Profession, and Degree .

5   And for thy Trecherie, what's more manifest ?
     In that thou layd'st a Trap to take my Life,
     As well at London Bridge, as at the Tower .

6   Beside, I feare me, if thy thoughts were sifted,

- it's fascinating that a man of such political acumen does not use a single debating colon anywhere in the speech

- it's also fascinating that the opening three F sentences display passion (7/7) rather than intellectual control, and that four of the final long spellings occur at the end of verse lines 4, 6, 7 and 8, suggesting that it is getting more and more difficult for him to retain a sense of dignified verbal control

- it is only by the middle of the speech (F #4-#5) that Gloster seems to regain mastery of himself, for as he lists his accusations of Winchester's personal faults and supposed crimes

  a. intellectual control finally takes over (11/3)

  b. each sentence contains a different set of accusations, F #4 decries Winchester's inner nature, while F #5 deals with Winchester's actions: as such, the two sentences have far more bite as separate indictments than the modern texts resetting them as just one (mt #4)

- but the control doesn't last, for in the final sentence, expressing fear for his beloved nephew's well-being, Gloster's personal feelings break through once more for a final passionate outburst (2/3)

The First Part of Henry the Sixt

Winchester

Gloster, I doe defie thee . Lords vouchsafe
3.1.27–40

Background: to repeat the opening of the background to the prior speech, 'in the struggle to become the power behind the current holder of the English throne, Henry VI, Henry's politically oriented uncle Humfrey, Duke of Gloster, and his great-uncle the churchman Henry Beaufort, Bishop of Winchester are at each other's throats, as are their respective supporters.' Here Gloster has publicly attacked (first by pamphlets and now in the open court) the Bishop for being a 'pernitious Usurer', for 'lewd, pestiferous, and dissentious prancks', and for 'Trecherie' in seeking Gloster's life (see prior speech). This is the Bishop's response.

Style: one on one for the benefit of a larger group

Where: the English Court

To Whom: Gloster, in front of Henry VI, Exeter, Warwicke, Somerset, Suffolk, and Yorke

# of Lines: 15

Probable Timing: 0.50 minutes

Take Note: While the sentence structure of both texts matches, F's orthography suggests a very different approach to the situation than Gloster displayed in the previous speech.

Winchester

1   [Gloucester], I do defy thee .

2   Lords, vouchsafe
To give me hearing what I shall reply .

3   If [ ] covetous, ambitious, or perverse,
As he will have me, how am I so poor ?

4   Or how haps it I seek not to advance
Or raise myself , but keep my wonted calling?

5   And for dissension, who preferreth peace
More [than] I do , except I be provok'd ?

6   No, my good lords, it is not that offends,
It is not that, that hath incens'd the Duke :
It is because no one should sway but he,
No one, but he, should be about the King ;
And that engenders thunder in his breast,
And makes him roar these accusations forth .

7   But he shall know I am as good—

Winchester

1   [Gloster], I doe defie thee .

2   Lords vouchsafe
     To give me hearing what I shall reply .

3   If [I were covetous], ambitious, or perverse,
     As he will have me : how am I so poore ?

4   Or how haps it, I seeke not to advance
     Or rayse my selfe ? but keepe my wonted Calling .

5   And for Dissention, who preferreth Peace
     More [then] I doe?x except I be provok'd .

6   No, my good Lords, it is not that offends,
     It is not that, that hath incens'd the Duke :
     It is because no one should sway but hee,
     No one, but hee, should be about the King ;
     And that engenders Thunder in his breast,
     And makes him rore these Accusations forth .

7   But he shall know I am as good .

- at first glance, Winchester seems so much calmer, especially in the opening three sentences (0/2)

- yet, in finishing defending himself (F sentence #4), suddenly personal feelings flash through (1/4 in just two lines), followed by a somewhat passionate though controlled recovery (sentence #5) as he describes himself as a man of peace (2/2, again in just two lines)

- the modern repunctuation of the last line of F #4 and #5 reduces the F Winchester's splendid oratorical trick of posing two questions and then answering them himself to a mere posing of the questions

- and though the start of F #6 suggests calm once more as Winchester begins to hint at what is disturbing Gloster, the last four lines of the sentence suggests that the calm may be somewhat of a mask, for both intellect and feeling break through (3/2) as he denigrates Gloster without actually answering his earlier and potent accusations, the final two lines are launched into via the only (emotional) semicolon in the speech

- so the calm of the final sentence is open to question: it could be a genuine return to a personal state of grace, or it could be deliberately engendered to win more debating points

The First Part of Henry the Sixt

Mortimer

With silence, Nephew, be thou pollitick,
between 2.5.100–114

Background: with his dying words, Mortimer counsels Yorke to maintain a 'pollitick' silence.

Style: as part of a two-handed scene

Where: the Tower of London

To Whom: Yorke, with perhaps Jaylers still onstage, and if so, whether they are privy to this conversation or no is up to each production to decide—though with Mortimer counselling caution, active listening on the Jaylers' part seems unlikely

# of Lines: 10

Probable Timing: 0.35 minutes

Take Note: The simple replacing of the comma at the end of F #1's first line with a modern period removes the urgency with which Mortimer begins to advise his nephew Richard, Duke of York. F's setting coupled with its orthography presents a different character than do the modern texts.

Mortimer

1 With silence, nephew, be thou politic .

2 Strong fixed is the house of Lancaster,
   And like a mountain, not to be remov'd .

3 But now thy uncle is removing hence,
   As princes do their courts, when they are cloy'd
   With long continuance in a settled place .

---

4 Mourn not, except thou sorrow for my good,
   Only give order for my funeral .

5 And so farewell, and fair be all thy hopes,
   And prosperous be thy life in peace and war !

Mortimer

1   With silence, Nephew, be thou pollitick,
      Strong fixed is the House of Lancaster,
      And like a Mountaine, not to be remov'd .

2   But now thy Unckle is removing hence,
      As Princes doe their Courts, when they are cloy'd
      With long continuance in a setled place .

---

3   Mourne not, except thou sorrow for my good,
      Onely give order for my Funerall .

4   And so farewell, and faire be all thy hopes,
      And prosperous be thy Life in Peace and Warre .

- the fact that there is no heavy punctuation accompanying the large scale intellectual and emotional release throughout the speech (11/9 in just 10 lines) suggests a heartfelt release with no thought of the fine-tuning of debate

- the passion of the political advice in first F sentence (4/2) spills into F #2 as Mortimer begins to make his farewells

- personal emotion breaks through unchecked in F #3 as the facts of death ('Mourne' and 'Funerall') are faced head-on (1/3), and then intellect is added to the last sentence as Mortimer offers a blessing to Richard (3/2)

The First Part of Henry the Sixt
Richard

Peace, no Warre, befall thy parting Soule.
2.5.115–129

Background: this is Richard, Duke of Yorke's farewell to his deceased uncle, Mortimer, and his vow to right the wrongs Somerset (Lancaster) has done to his house.

Style: initially a funereal address in front of a small group, and then solo

Where: the Tower of London

To Whom: the first four sentences to the dead Mortimer as he is carried out by the Jaylers, the last three to himself and the audience

# of Lines: 15

Probable Timing: 0.50 minutes

Take Note: The modern texts' jamming together of F's sentences #5-#6 minimises the very emphatic way York vows to regain his family's honour and (as it turns out) his fateful decision to advance his claim to the throne. F's setting, plus its orthography, presents a man at one and the same time both moved and highly determined.

Richard

1   {† P}eace, no war, befall thy parting soul !

2   In prison hast thou spent a pilgrimage,
     And like a hermit over-past thy days .

3   Well, I will lock [his] counsel in my breast,
     And what I do imagine, let that rest .

4   Keepers, convey him hence, and I myself
     Will see his burial better [than] his life .
                    [Exit Attendants with the body of Mortimer]

5   Here dies the dusky torch of Mortimer,
     Chok'd with ambition of the meaner sort ;
     And for those wrongs, those bitter injuries,
     Which Somerset hath offer'd to my house,
     I doubt not but with honor to redress .

6   And therefore haste I to the parliament,
     Either to be restored to my blood,
     Or make my will th'advantage of my good .

Richard

1   {† P}eace, no Warre, befall thy parting Soule .

2   In Prison hast thou spent a Pilgrimage,
     And like a Hermite over-past thy dayes .

3   Well, I will locke [this] Councell in my Brest,
     And what I doe imagine, let that rest .

4   Keepers convey him hence, and I my selfe
     Will see his Buryall better [then] his Life .
                    [Exit]

5   Here dyes the duskie Torch of Mortimer,
     Choakt with Ambition of the meaner sort .

6   And for those Wrongs, those bitter Injuries,
     Which Somerset hath offer'd to my House,
     I doubt not, but with Honor to redresse .

7   And therefore haste I to the Parliament,
     Eyther to be restored to my Blood,
     Or make my will th'advantage of my good .

- his mind is on high alert throughout (19 capitals scattered throughout 12 of the 15 lines of the speech)

- it is both his mind and personal feelings that are released in the first five F sentences, all focused on his just deceased uncle Mortimer and his advice (12/11 in 9 lines)

- and then, as he gets down to business and makes his vow, unnecessary emotions are put aside (5/1 in F sentence #6), and, as he plans his next move, passion returns once more (2/1 in the first two lines of F #7)

The Second Part of Henry the Sixt
Cardinall

So, there goes our Protector in a rage :
1.1.147–171

Background: the churchman Beauford (known under the prefix 'Winchester' in *Henry The Sixth, Part One*), now promoted to Cardinall, has long been Gloster's sworn enemy (see prior speeches on pages 33 and 37, both the background to and the speeches of Winchester and Gloster). This is his undermining response once Gloster has exited (following his passionate outburst over Suffolkes arrangement of the insulting Margaret-Henry marriage agreement.

Style: as part of a six-handed scene

Where: the English court

To Whom: Salisbury, Warwicke, Yorke, Somerset, and Buckingham

# of Lines: 25

Probable Timing: 1.15 minutes

Take Note: The supposed intellectual control of the eleven sentence modern text Cardinall is in no way the character set up in the five sentences of F, especially with F's long eleven-line onrushed anti-Gloster sentence #1 being broken down into a more considered, rational mt. five sentences. Similarly, modern texts split F #2 in two, reducing even further the oratorical intensity and build of the Cardinall's anti-Gloster diatribe

Cardinall

1   So, there goes our Protector in a rage .

2   'Tis known to you he is mine enemy ;
    Nay more, an enemy unto you all,
    And no great friend, I fear me, to the King .

3   Consider, lords, he is the next of blood,
    And heir-apparent to the English crown .

4   Had Henry got an empire by his marriage,
    And all the wealthy kingdoms of the west,
    There's reason he should be displeas'd at it .

5   Look to it, lords, let not his smoothing words
    Bewitch your hearts .

6   Be wise and circumspect .

7   What though the common people favor him,
    Calling him, "[Humphrey], the good Duke of
                                [Gloucester,]"
    Clapping their hands, and crying with loud voice,
    "Jesu maintain your Royal Excellence !"
    With "God preserve the good Duke [Humphrey]!"

8   I fear me, lords, for all this flattering gloss,
    He will be found a dangerous Protector .

9 {†} Why should he then protect our sovereign ,
    He being of age to govern of himself ?

10 Cousin of Somerset, join you with me,
    And [all together], with the Duke of Suffolk,
    We'll quickly hoise Duke [Humphrey] from his seat .

11 {†} This weighty business will not brook delay,
    I'll to the Duke of Suffolk presently .

Cardinall

1　So, there goes our Protector in a rage :
　'Tis knowne to you he is mine enemy :
　Nay more, an enemy unto you all,
　And no great friend, I feare me to the King ;
　Consider Lords, he is the next of blood,
　And heyre apparant to the English Crowne :
　Had Henrie got an Empire by his marriage,
　And all the wealthy Kingdomes of the West,
　There's reason he should be displeas'd at it :
　Looke to it Lords, let not his smoothing words
　Bewitch your hearts, be wise and circumspect .

2　What though the common people favour him,
　Calling him, [[Humfrey] the good Duke of [Gloster],
　Clapping their hands, and crying with loud voyce,
　Jesu maintaine your Royall Excellence,
　With God preserve the good Duke [Humfrey] :
　I feare me Lords, for all this flattering glosse,
　He will be found a dangerous Protector .

3 {t} Why should he then protect our Soveraigne ?
　He being of age to governe of himselfe .

4　Cosin of Somerset, joyne you with me,
　And [altogether] with the Duke of Suffolke,
　Wee'l quickly hoyse Duke [Humfrey] from his seat .

5{t} This weighty businesse will not brooke delay,
　Ile to the Duke of Suffolke presently .

- not only does the unusually heavy major punctuation opening the speech betray the Cardinall's working so hard from the outset to gain the advantage over Gloster, but the large number of surround phrases so created clearly demonstrates, above all else, the personal enmity which is the basis for the Cardinall's attack

- the single (emotional) semicolon (F #1, line 4) begins to hint at the factually-correct-leading-to-the-illogical-libelous-implication   that Gloster might be 'no great friend . . to the King', viz. " ; Consider Lords, he is the next of blood,"

- there are at least five occasions (marked '') where modern texts have added extra punctuation not originally set by F thus slowing down the faster (more determined?) release (e.g. lines 4 and 5 of sentence #1)

- though it seems the Cardinall is in strident mode throughout the speech (28/21 in 25 lines), it is fascinating to note how the long spellings build

  a. just 6 in the first eleven lines of F #1

  b. 6 in the seven lines of sentence #2

  c. and finally, as he begins to voice the plot to remove Gloster from his all powerful role as Protector of the realm, there are, for the first time in the speech, more long spellings (9) than lines (7)

The Third Part of Henry the Sixt

Yorke

Bidst thou me rage ?why now thou hast thy wish .
between 1.4.143–168

Background: Margaret has taunted the now captured Yorke to the best of her ability, in an effort to break his spirit before killing him. She has even shown him the blood of his youngest child Rutland whom she has had killed, but she has failed to bring him to tears or loss of self-control. Having given the command for Yorke to be killed, but slowly, the following speech forms his reply. As Yorke finally faces up to the death of Rutland, he gives way to tears—seemingly giving Margaret what she has worked so hard for.

Style: essentially a one on one address for the benefit of the larger group

Where: the battlefield

To Whom: Margaret, her son the young Prince of Wales, Clifford, Northumberland, and Lancastrian soldiers

# of Lines: 25

Probable Timing: 1.15 minutes

Take Note: Once more F's orthography and sentence structure reveal much about Yorke's dignity and humanity. In this, speech, Yorke is quickly overtaken by passion.

York

1　Bid'st thou me rage ?why, now thou hast thy wish :
　Would'st have me weep ?why, now thou hast thy will :
　For raging wind blows up incessant showers,
　And when the rage allays, the rain begins .

2　These tears are my sweet Rutland's obsequies,
　And every drop cries vengeance for his death
　'Gainst thee, fell Clifford, and thee, false French-woman .

3　That face of his the hungry cannibals
　Would not have touch'd, would not have stain'd with
　　　　　　　　　　　　　　　　　　　　blood ;
　But you are more [inhuman], more inexorable,
　O, ten times more, [than] tigers of Hyrcania .

4　See, ruthless queen, a hapless father's tears !

5　This cloth thou dippd'st in blood of my sweet boy,
　And I with tears do wash the blood away .

6　Keep thou the napkin and go boast of this,
　And if thou tell'st the heavy story right,
　Upon my soul, the hearers will shed tears;
　Yea, even my foes will shed fast-falling tears,
　And say, "Alas, it was a piteous deed !"

7　There, take the crown, and with the crown, my curse,
　And in thy need such comfort come to thee
　As now I reap at thy too cruel hand !

8　Hard-hearted Clifford, take me from the world,
　My soul to heaven, my blood upon your heads !

Yorke

1　Bidst thou me rage ?why now thou hast thy wish .

2　Would'st have me weepe ?why now thou hast thy will .

3　For raging Wind blowes up incessant showers,
　And when the Rage allayes, the Raine begins .

4　These Teares are my sweet Rutlands Obsequies,
　And every drop cryes vengeance for his death,
　'Gainst thee fell Clifford, and thee false French-woman .

5　That Face of his,
　　　　　The hungry Caniballs would not have toucht,
　Would not have stayn'd with blood :
　But you are more [inhumane], more inexorable,
　Oh, tenne times more [then] Tygers of Hyrcania .

6　See, ruthlesse Queene, a haplesse Fathers Teares :
　This Cloth thou dipd'st in blood of my sweet Boy,
　And I with Teares doe wash the blood away .

7　Keepe thou the Napkin, and goe boast of this,
　And if thou tell'st the heavie storie right,
　Upon my Soule, the hearers will shed Teares :
　Yea, even my Foes will shed fast-falling Teares,
　And say, Alas, it was a pittious deed .

8　There, take the Crowne, and with the Crowne, my Curse,
　And in thy need, such comfort come to thee,
　As now I reape at thy too cruell hand .

9　Hard-hearted Clifford, take me from the World,
　My Soule to Heaven, my Blood upon your Heads .

- the dangerous calm in which this speech starts is enhanced in the two unusually short F sentences #1-2, with virtually no embellishment (0/1) and both monosyllabic

- as Yorke starts to 'rage' so passion is released (F #3-4, 8/5)—in so doing the last line of the F text moves much faster without the two extra modern text commas (marked)

- as he begins to talk of his murdered child F #5 opens with three irregular lines (4/10/6 syllables), suggesting that Yorke is having great difficulty forming his thoughts at such a dreadful point: most modern texts wipe this out by setting the start as two regular lines

- and compared with the previous speech, the passion now rolls on unchecked as he denies the Queene her moment of victory, suggesting that he will be better remembered this day than she—and this lasts through both giving her the 'Crowne' and his 'Curse' (19/20 in the fourteen lines from F #5 to the first line of #8)

- the last four lines of the speech shows three interesting states

  a. as he fleshes out his curse 'And in thy need, such comfort come to thee', he becomes deadly calm, with no embellishment—but the strain thus involved manifests itself in the two extra breath-thoughts the line contains (as if he needs the extra breaths both to stay in control and to make sure she understands each point)

  b. but in the last line of F #8 detailing the curse, emotions get the better of him for just a moment (0/2)

  c. then, as he invites death (F #9), he regains intellectual discipline (6/1 in just two lines)

The Third Part of Henry the Sixt
Warwicke

From worthy Edward, King of Albion,
between 3.3.49–64

Background: unaware that King Edward has already married the impoverished English widow Lady Gray, the Yorkist Warwicke has arrived at the court of the French King Lewis to propose a league of 'amitie' supposedly to be sealed by marriage between Edward and Lewis' sister, the Lady Bona. What makes the scene even more interesting is that he interrupts a plea by the Lancastrian Margaret for French aid to continue the civil war against the Yorkists.

Style: public address in front of a large group

Where: the French Court

To Whom: the King of France and his sister Lady Bona, in front of his Admiral, the Lancastrian Margaret, Margaret's son, and her supporter Oxford

# of Lines: 15

Probable Timing: 0.55 minutes

Take Note: The structure of the texts match, thus the value of F lies in its emphasis on certain aspects of what is a very rhetorical public address.

Warwicke

1   From worthy Edward, King of Albion,
    My lord and sovereign and thy vowed friend,
    I come, in kindness and unfeigned love,
    First, to do greetings to thy royal person,
    And then to crave a league of amity,
    And lastly, to confirm that amity
    With nuptial knot, if thou vouchsafe to grant
    That virtuous Lady Bona, thy fair sister,
    To England's king in lawful marriage .

---

2   And gracious {Lady Bona,} in our king's behalf
    I am commanded, with your leave and favor,
    Humbly to kiss your hand, and with my tongue
    To tell the passion of my sovereign's heart,
    Where fame, late ent'ring at his heedful ears,
    Hath plac'd thy beauty's image and thy virtue .

Warwicke

1 From worthy Edward, King of Albion,
   My Lord and Soveraigne, and thy vowed Friend,
   I come (in Kindnesse, and unfayned Love)
   First, to doe greetings to thy Royall Person,
   And then to crave a League of Amitie :
   And lastly, to confirme that Amitie
   With Nuptiall Knot, if thou vouchsafe to graunt
   That vertuous Lady Bona, thy faire Sister,
   To Englands King, in lawfull Marriage .

---

2 And gracious {Lady Bona,} in our Kings behalfe,
   I am commanded, with your leave and favor,
   Humbly to kisse your Hand, and with my Tongue
   To tell the passion of my Soveraignes Heart ;
   Where Fame, late entring at his heedfull Eares,
   Hath plac'd thy Beauties Image, and thy Vertue .

- as an opening to alliance-through-marriage negotiations the fact that capitals (33) outweighing long-spellings (17) is hardly surprising

- what F does via punctuation, not followed in most modern texts, is to subtly divide each sentence into two parts

- thus in F #1 the offer of marriage (line 6 and on) is preceded by an F only colon, as if to heighten the anticipation and thus underscore the offer

- and the final flourish of praise to lady Bona herself (F #2) is preceded by a similar F only (emotional) semicolon: whether Warwicke is genuinely emotional or oratorically disingenuously so is up to each actor to explore

- even the three F only extra breath thoughts (marked ,) have their oratorical value

  a. the final praise of Lady Bona is enhanced by the F only extra comma in the last line, 'thy Beauties Image, and thy Vertue.'

  b. and the two extra commas in lines 2-3 of the speech serve to emphasise the second flattering part of each line 'and thy vowed Friend', & 'and unfayned Love'

The Third Part of Henry the Sixt
Warwicke

Heere is the Duke . I, when you disgrac'd me ...
between 4.3.29–57

Background: in the continually fluctuating and topsy-turvey world of 'now the Lancastrian Henry is King, and now the Yorkist Edward is', with the added French support, and especially since the ex-Yorkist Warwicke has switched sides to join their cause, the Lancastrian fortunes have improved enormously. So much so that, under Warwicke's guidance, the Yorkist King Edward has just been taken prisoner. Warwicke, once Edward's right-hand man, leaves the once-King-now-just-Duke-of-Yorke Edward in no doubt about how the French wooing fiasco (see prior speech) affected him.

Style: one on one in front of a small, and then larger, group

Where: Edward's camp

To Whom: Edward, in front of Oxford, Somerset, French Soldiers, and Edward's younger brother George, currently fighting against him on the Lancastrian side

# of Lines: 19

Probable Timing: 1.00 minutes

Take Note: F not only underscores the triumph of Warwicke's vow, it also hints at how his triumph is celebrated and almost runs away with him.

Warwick

1   {H}ere is the Duke .

---

2   Ay, when you disgrac'd me in my embassade,
     Then I degraded you for being king,
     And come now to create you Duke of York .

3   Alas, how should you govern any kingdom,
     That know not how to use ambassadors,
     Nor how to be contented with one wife,
     Nor how to use your brother's brotherly,
     Nor how to study for the people's welfare,
     Nor how to shroud your self from enemies?

---

4 {†} Henry now shall wear the English crown,
     And be true king indeed, thou but the shadow .

5   My Lord of Somerset, at my request,
     See that forthwith Duke Edward be convey'd
     Unto my brother, ArchBishop of York.

6   When I have fought with Pembroke and his fellows,
     I'll follow you, and [come] tell what answer
     Lewis and the Lady Bona send to him .

7   Now for a-while farewell, good Duke of York .

Warwicke

1   {H}eere is the Duke .

---

2   I, when you disgrac'd me in my Embassade,
      Then I degraded you for being King,
      And come now to create you Duke of Yorke .

3   Alas, how should you governe any Kingdome,
      That know not how to use Embassadors,
      Nor how to be contented with one Wife,
      Nor how to use your Brothers Brotherly,
      Nor how to studie for the Peoples Welfare,
      Nor how to shrowd your selfe from Enemies?

---

4 {†} Henry now shall weare the English Crowne,
      And be true King indeede : thou but the shadow .

5   My Lord of Somerset, at my request,
      See that forthwith Duke Edward be convey'd
      Unto my Brother Arch-Bishop of Yorke :
      When I have fought with Pembrooke, and his fellowes,
      Ile follow you, and [ ] tell what answer
      Lewis and the Lady Bona send to him .

6   Now for a-while farewell good Duke of Yorke .

- the one surround phrase ' : thou but the shadow . ' sums up how successfully Warwicke has accomplished what he intended to achieve

- with capitals (31) vastly outweighing long-spellings (14) in just nineteen lines, it seems that the triumph is one of mind more than spirit, or that the mind can hold the joy in check—certainly this would explain the long listing of what Edward is being stripped of (F #3)

- F's onrushed #5, juxtaposing the imprisonment of Edward with Warwicke's need to defeat some of Edward's supporters before humiliating Edward further, suggests more urgency (and possibly confident, even over-confident, excitement) than the modern texts maintain, that usually split F #5 into two

The Tragedy of Richard the Third
Hastings

Goe fellow, goe, returne unto thy Lord,
3.2.19–33

Background: Stanley, Hastings' fellow counselor, has dreamt, as it turns out correctly, that Richard is about to go on a murderous spree and that both Stanley and Hastings are in danger. Thus Stanley has sent a warning to Hastings who cavalierly dismisses the messenger with the following, at the eventual cost of his life (see speech immediately following). One note; the repetition of the 'Bore', sentence #3, is a direct reference to Richard via the emblem of a 'boar' on his coat of arms.

Style: as part of a two-handed scene

Where: unspecified, possibly outside the house of Hastings' lover, Mistress Shore

To Whom: to a messenger sent from his friend Stanley

# of Lines: 15

Probable Timing: 0.50 minutes

Take Note: While the sentence structure of the two texts match, F's orthography shows two different facets of Hastings presumption of safety.

Hastings

1   Go, fellow, go, return unto thy lord,
    Bid him not fear the separated Council:
    His honor and myself are at the one,
    And at the other is my good friend Catesby ;
    Where nothing can proceed that toucheth us
    Whereof I shall not have intelligence .

2   Tell him his fears are shallow, without instance ;
    And for his dreams, I wonder he's so simple
    To trust the mock'ry of unquiet slumbers .

3   To fly the boar before the boar pursues
    Were to incense the boar to follow us,
    And make pursuit where he did mean no chase .

4   Go, bid thy master rise and come to me,
    And we will both together to the Tower,
    Where he shall see the boar will use us kindly .

Hastings

1   Goe fellow, goe, returne unto thy Lord,
      Bid him not feare the seperated Councell :
      His Honor and my selfe are at the one,
      And at the other, is my good friend Catesby ;
      Where nothing can proceede, that toucheth us,
      Whereof I shall not have intelligence :
      Tell him his Feares are shallow, without instance .

2   And for his Dreames, I wonder hee's so simple,
      To trust the mock'ry of unquiet slumbers .

3   To flye the Bore, before the Bore pursues,
      Were to incense the Bore to follow us,
      And make pursuit, where he did meane no chase .

4   Goe, bid thy Master rise, and come to me,
      And we will both together to the Tower,
      Where he shall see the Bore will use us kindly .

- the overconfidence of Hastings can be seen in the two non-embellished lines

  a. that (because of his 'good friend Catesby;') nothing untoward could happen 'Whereof I shall not have intelligence'

  b. and thus how foolish it is 'To trust the mock'ry of unquiet slumbers.'

- the speech seems to split into two parts, the passionate/emotional F #1-2 dismissal of Stanley's fears (6/10 in nine lines); and F #3-4's more intellectual explanation of the plan to go to London, and how dangerous it would be 'To flye the Bore', i.e. Richard, (6/3)

- it's interesting that the three major punctuations are all used to dismiss Stanley's fears (perhaps suggesting Hastings' passion is backed by determined argument), and three of the extra breath-thoughts (marked ,) are needed to heighten the explanations of why not to flee, F #3

- of the three pieces of heavy punctuation, the only emotional semicolon deals with the (incorrect) warranty as to the value and loyalty of Catesby

The Tragedy of Richard the Third
Hastings

Woe, woe for England, not a whit for me,
between 3.4.80–107

Background: already somewhat suspicious of Hastings' loyalty, Richard, following the deaths of his brothers Edward and George (Clarence), had Catesby sound Hastings out as to whether Richard should be King, to which Hastings replied unequivocally 'Ile have this Crown of mine cut frō my shoulders,/Before Ile see the Crowne so foule mis-plac'd'. As a result, Hastings has been arrested on a trumped-up charge of conspiracy by witchcraft (supposedly causing Richard's withered arm). These are Hastings' final words before being escorted to execution.

Style: as part of a two or three-handed scene

Where: a meeting room in the Tower of London

To Whom: either Lovell and Ratcliffe (First Folio), or just Catesby (quartos)

# of Lines: 25

Probable Timing: 1.15 minutes

Take Note: F's sentence structure, altered by most modern texts at the beginning and end of the speech, suggests that while Hastings has a good mental grip on what is happening to him (with the logic of four colons, and 28 capitals to 20 long spellings), the strain he is undergoing is considerable.

Hastings

1 Woe, woe for England, not a whit for me !

2 For I, too fond, might have prevented this .

3 Stanley did dream the boar did [rase] our helms,
   And I did scorn it and disdain to fly .

4 Three times to day my foot-cloth horse did stumble,
   And started when he look'd upon the Tower,
   As loath to bear me to the slaughter-house .

5 O now I need the priest that spake to me !

6 I now repent I told the pursuivant,
   As too triumphing, how mine enemies
   To day at Pomfret bloodily were butcher'd,
   And I myself secure, in grace and favor .

7 O Margaret, Margaret, now thy heavy curse
   Is lighted on poor Hasting's wretched head !

---

8 O momentary grace of mortal men,
   Which we more hunt for [than] the grace of God !

9 Who builds his hope in air of your good looks
   Lives like a drunken sailor on a mast,
   Ready with every nod to tumble down
   Into the fatal bowels of the deep .

---

10 O bloody Richard !

11   Miserable England !

12 I prophesy the fearfull'st time to thee
    That ever wretched age hath look'd upon .

13 Come, lead me to the block, bear him my head .

14 They smile at me who shortly shall be dead .

Hastings

1　Woe, woe for England, not a whit for me,
　For I, too fond, might have prevented this :
　Stanley did dreame, the Bore did [rowse] our Helmes,
　And I did scorne it, and disdaine to flye :
　Three times to day my Foot-Cloth-Horse did stumble,
　And started, when he look'd upon the Tower,
　As loth to beare me to the slaughter-house .

2　O now I need the Priest, that spake to me :
　I now repent I told the Pursuivant,
　As too triumphing, how mine Enemies
　To day at Pomfret bloodily were butcher'd,
　And I my selfe secure, in grace and favour .

3　Oh Margaret, Margaret, now thy heavie Curse
　Is lighted on poore Hastings wretched Head .

4　O momentarie grace of mortall men,
　Which we more hunt for, [then] the grace of God !

5　Who builds his hope in ayre of your good Lookes,
　Lives like a drunken Sayler on a Mast,
　Readie with every Nod to tumble downe,
　Into the fatall Bowels of the Deepe .

6　O bloody Richard : miserable England,
　I prophecie the fearefull'st time to thee,
　That ever wretched Age hath look'd upon .

7　Come, lead me to the Block, beare him my Head,
　They smile at me, who shortly shall be dead .

- the onrush of F #1, connecting as it does thoughts for the good of England with Stanley's warning and the morning's omens that he ignored, suggests a mind fighting to avoid being swamped: most modern texts split the speech into four separate parts

- and the slight onrush of F #2, combining the need for the Priest he met that morning with an act of contrition for what he bragged of that morning, is also split in two by most modern texts

- the two surround phrases
  " . O now I need the Priest, that spake to me : " & " . O bloody Richard : "
  suggest the basis from which the speech stems

- the mental control with which Hastings' opens the speech, F #1, (the first two lines, 1/0, and the last three lines plus all but the last line of F #2, 8/1) doesn't always last and cannot always be sustained, for

- the mention of Stanley's prescient warning dream triggers an enormous emotional response (3/5 in just the 3rd and 4th line of F #1)

- and, with the last line of F #2, as the irony of describing himself that very morning as 'secure, in grace and favour' hits home, so emotion is released again (0/2 in the one line)

- Hastings then regains some intellectual discipline as he now sees how Margaret's curse has lighted on him (F #3, 5/2)

- which turns to passion as he realises the fragility of seeking for 'grace' in the world of men (7/7 in the six lines of F #4-5)

- but in the final moments, calling out Richard for what he is and the pain he will bring to 'miserable England' (F #6), and taking control of the march to execution (F #7), his sense of mental discipline returns (5/2 in all)

- there is also more release and inevitability in both F #6 and #7 as separate sentences, as if nothing is being held back: modern texts have reduced the impact of both by splitting them (F #6 into three, F #7 into two)

The Life and Death of King John
King John

Sirra, your brother is Legittimate,
1.1.116–129

Background: in response to Robert's plea (speech #1 above), John rules against him in favour of his brother Philip.

Style: one on one address in full view and hearing of a larger group

Where: the palace

To Whom: Robert Faulconbridge, in front of Robert's brother Philip, John's mother Eleanor, the lords Pembroke, Essex, and Salisbury, and a 'Sheriffe'

# of Lines: 14

Probable Timing: 0.45 minutes

Take Note: Unlike the modern texts' rational response, F seems to give John an onrushed and emotional reply—suggesting amusement perhaps?, or even anger. Certainly F is far less formal than the dignified rationality the modern texts offer by splitting the one F sentence into four.

King John

1　Sirrah, your brother is legitimate,
　Your father's wife did after wedlock bear him ;
　And if she did play false, the fault was hers,
　Which fault lies on the hazards of all husbands
　That marry wives .

2　　　　　　　　　　Tell me, how if my brother,
　Who as you say, took pains to get this son,
　Had of your father claim'd this son for his ?

3　In sooth, good friend, your father might have kept
　This calf , bred from his cow from all the world ;
　In sooth he might ; then if he were my brother's,
　My brother might not claim him, nor your father,
　Being none of his, refuse him .

4　　　　　　　　　　This concludes,
　My mother's son did get your father's heir;
　Your father's heir must have your father's land .

King John

1   Sirra, your brother is Legittimate,
    Your fathers wife did after wedlocke beare him :
    And if she did play false, the fault was hers,
    Which fault lyes on the hazards of all husbands
    That marry wives : tell me, how if my brother
    Who as you say, tooke paines to get this sonne,
    Had of your father claim'd this sonne for his,
    Insooth, good friend, your father might have kept
    This Calfe, bred from his Cow from all the world :
    Insooth he might : then if he were my brothers,
    My brother might not claime him, nor your father
    Being none of his, refuse him : this concludes,
    My mothers sonne did get your fathers heyre,
    Your fathers heyre must have your fathers land .

- because the one long sentence reply is neatly divided into logical component parts by the five colons, it seems that John answers well the points raised by Robert: however, fourteen lines without the need of a new sentence also suggests that the answer flows out of him very easily

- the key point, that Robert's father might have denied Robert's brother Phillip as his own son, but didn't, is emphasised in the one surround phrase in the speech, ' : Insooth he might : '

- while the content is quite rational, the whole is full of personal feelings (3/12), somewhat unexpected when considering the absolute rationality of the reply

- two of the three capitalised words ('Calfe' and 'Cow') deal with the matter in a humorous, if coarsely demeaning, way—perhaps a sign of how seriously (or otherwise) John regards the matter, and perhaps too a clue to his character

The Life and Death of King Richard the Second

Mowbray

A heavy sentence, my most Soveraigne Liege,

between 1.3.154–177

Background: these are the final words of Thomas Mowbray, Duke of Norfolke, after Richard has sentenced him to permanent exile from England (following Richard's intervention to stop the trial by combat between Mowbrary and Henry Bolingbroke).

Style: one on one address in front of a larger public group at an outdoors event

Where: the lists at Coventry

To Whom: Richard, in front of Mowbray's fellow combatant Bullingbrooke, the Lord Marshall, the nobles Bushy, Bagot, Greene, 'others' including Bullingbrooke's father John of Gaunt, and heralds

# of Lines: 22

Probable Timing: 1.10 minutes

Take Note: Mowbray's response to his banishment is far less rhetorically controlled than most modern texts would suggest, especially with the onrushed sentence F #1 which, as set is an unconstrained initial response rather than the well argued two sentence rebuke set by most modern texts. Similarly, the onrush of F #3 suggests a man releasing his loss rather than making a dignified assessment of what is to come, as modern texts tend to express it—by splitting it in three.

Mowbray

1   A heavy sentence, my most sovereign liege,
    And all unlook'd for from your Highness' mouth .

2   A dearer merit, not so deep a maim
    As to be cast forth in the common air
    Have I deserved at your Highness' hands .

3   The language I have learnt these forty years,
    My native English, now I must forgo,
    And now my tongue's use is to me no more
    [Than] an unstringed [viol] or a harp,
    Or like a cunning instrument cas'd up,
    Or being open, put into his hands
    That knows no touch to tune the harmony .

4   Within my mouth you have enjail'd my tongue,
    Doubly [portcullis'd] with my teeth and lips,
    And dull unfeeling barren ignorance
    Is made my jailor to attend on me .

5   I am too old to fawn upon a nurse,
    Too far in years to be a pupil now .

6   What is thy sentence then but speechless death,
    Which robs my tongue from breathing native breath ?

7   Then thus I turn me from my country's light,
    To dwell in solemn shades of endless night .

Mowbray

1   A heavy sentence, my most Soveraigne Liege,
      And all unlook'd for from your Highnesse mouth :
      A deerer merit, not so deepe a maime,
      As to be cast forth in the common ayre
      Have I deserved at your Highnesse hands .

2   The Language I have learn'd these forty yeares
      (My native English) now I must forgo,
      And now my tongues use is to me no more,
      [Then] an unstringed [Vyall], or a Harpe,
      Or like a cunning Instrument cas'd up,
      Or being open, put into his hands
      That knowes no touch to tune the harmony .

3   Within my mouth you have engaol'd my tongue,
      Doubly [percullist] with my teeth and lippes,
      And dull, unfeeling, barren ignorance,
      Is made my Gaoler to attend on me :
      I am too old to fawne upon a Nurse,
      Too farre in yeeres to be a pupill now :
      What is thy sentence then, but speechlesse death,
      Which robs my tongue from breathing native breath ?

4   Then thus I turne me from my countries light
      To dwell in solemne shades of endlesse night.

- the non-embellished lines show the enormity of what Mowbray now faces

  "And now my tongues use is to me no more,"

  "Within my mouth you have engaol'd my tongue"

  "Which robs my tongue from breathing native breath"

- therefore it is not surprising that F #1 starts out as more of a blurt than as shown in most modern texts, and passionately at first (3/2 in the first two lines), becoming highly emotional (1/5 in the remaining three lines of F #1)

- and while the passion remains, it is not quite as manifest during most of the rest of the speech, as at first it seems that Mowbray manages to get control of his emotions (just 5/4 in the seven lines of F #2; but then lack of control creeps back in, for while there are just three emotional releases in five of the eight lines of the onrushed F #3 there is still the blurt (2/5) contained in lines 4 through 6

- the two moments when emotions get the better of him are very telling,

  " I am too old to fawne upon a Nurse,/Too farre in yeeres to be a pupill now : " (1/4)

  and the final sentence as he leaves

  "Then thus I turne me from my countries light /To dwell in solemne shades of endlesse night ." (0/3)

The Life and Death of King Richard the Second
Gaunt

{'Tis thou that} dyest, though I the sicker be .
between 2.1.91–116

Background: Richard and his coterie have finally arrived to see his
dying uncle. After some pointed bickering and puns over the name
of 'Gaunt', Gaunt finally begins his extremely blunt 'wholesome
counsell'.

Style: one on one in front of a larger group who cannot avoid listening

Where: Gaunt's quarters

To Whom: King Richard, in front of the Duke of Yorke, and
Richard's entourage including the Queene, Bushy, Bagot, Greene,
Ross, Willoughby, and attendants

# of Lines: 23

Probable Timing: 1.10 minutes

Take Note: While F's onrushed sentence structure shows Gaunt los-
ing some self-control, F's orthography shows his remarkable determination to make his points heard.

Gaunt

1 {'Tis thou that} diest, though I the sicker be .

2 {†} He that made me, knows I see thee ill :
   Ill in myself to see, and in thee, seeing ill .

3 Thy death-bed is no lesser [than] [thy] land,
   Wherein thou liest in reputation sick,
   And thou too careless patient as thou art,
   Commit'st thy'anointed body to the cure
   Of those physicians that first wounded thee .

4 A thousand flatterers sit within thy crown,
   Whose compass is no bigger [than] thy head,
   And yet incaged in so small a verge,
   The waste is no whit lesser [than] thy land .

5 O had thy grandsire with a prophet's eye,
   Seen how his son's son should destroy his sons,
   From forth thy reach he would have laid thy shame,
   Deposing thee before thou wert posses'd,
   Which art posses'd now to depose thyself .

6 Why, cousin, [wert] thou regent of the world,
   It were a shame to let [this] land by lease ;
   But for thy world enjoying but this land,
   Is it not more [than] shame, to shame it so ?

7 Landlord of England art thou [now], and not king,
   Thy state of law is bond-slave to the law,
   And ———————

Gaunt

1 {'Tis thou that} dyest, though I the sicker be .

---

2 {†} He that made me, knowes I see thee ill :
　　Ill in my selfe to see, and in thee, seeing ill,
　　Thy death-bed is no lesser [then] [the] Land,
　　Wherein thou lyest in reputation sicke,
　　And thou too care-lesse patient as thou art,
　　Commit'st thy'anointed body to the cure
　　Of those Physitians, that first wounded thee .

3 A thousand flatterers sit within thy Crowne,
　　Whose compasse is no bigger [then] thy head,
　　And yet incaged in so small a Verge,
　　The waste is no whit lesser [then] thy Land :
　　Oh had thy Grandsire with a Prophets eye,
　　Seene how his sonnes sonne, should destroy his sonnes,
　　From forth thy reach he would have laid thy shame,
　　Deposing thee before thou wert possest,
　　Which art possest now to depose thy selfe .

4 Why (Cosine) [were] thou Regent of the world,
　　It were a shame to let [his] Land by lease :
　　But for thy world enjoying but this Land,
　　Is it not more [then] shame, to shame it so ?

5 Landlord of England art thou [ ], and not King :
　　Thy state of Law, is bondslave to the law,
　　And ————————

- the three surround phrases provide the spine of Gaunt's attack

    " . He that made me knowes I see thee ill : ", and

    " . Landlord of England art thou, and not King : /Thy state of
    Law, is bondslave to the law,/And—"

- while three of the non-embellished lines point out how Richard's acts
  despoil both the memory of his illustrious Grandfather, Edward III

    "From forth thy reach he would have laid thy shame,/Deposing
    thee before thou wert possest,"

  and the land itself

    "Is it not more then shame, to shame it so?"

- the opening, magnified by the unusual one sentence start (presumably signifying that the gloves are off as he then elaborates how
  Richard can figuratively can be justly said to be on his 'death-bed')
  is virtually all emotional (2/6, F #1-2): and the onrush heightens his
  attack—most modern texts split F #2 into two grammatically correct sentences, (the first two lines—Gaunt sick—as mt. #2 and then
  a new sentence, mt. #3, for Richard's 'sickness')

- F's onrushed attack continues via F #3, and as Gaunt pours scorn on
  Richard's flatterers, his intellect takes over, even if only momentarily
  (5/2 in the first four lines)

- but then as the honour of Richard's grandfather is voiced, so the remainder of the sentence becomes highly emotional (1/5 in just two
  lines), the onrush of this removed by most modern texts which start
  their new mt. #5 here

- F #3 then becomes deadly calm as two non-embellished lines essentially express the thought that Richard really deserves to be deposed

- amazingly, the speech ends with tremendous mental discipline as
  Gaunt tells Richard to his face just how low he has sunk (7/1 in six
  lines)

The Life and Death of King Richard the Second
Gaunt

Oh spare me not, my brothers Edwards sonne,
2.1.124–138

Background: instead of doing any good, Gaunt's dying words infuriate Richard to the point of calling his uncle 'a lunaticke leane-witted foole,/Presuming on Ague's priviledge', bluntly informing him that 'Were't thou not Brother to great Edwards sonne,/This tongue that runs so roundly in thy head,/Should run thy head from thy unreverent shoulders'; all of which triggers the following reply.

Style: one on one in front of a larger group who cannot avoid listening

Where: Gaunt's quarters

To Whom: King Richard, in front of the Duke of Yorke, and Richard's entourage including the Queene, Bushy, Bagot, Greene, Ross, Willoughby, and attendants

# of Lines: 15

Probable Timing: 0.50 minutes

Take Note: That Gaunt expends an enormous amount of energy in standing up to his nephew can be seen in the totally unenergised, death-anticipating, last sentence ending (F #4): "Convey me to my bed, then to my grave, /Love they to live, that love and honor have ."

Gaunt

1   O, spare me not, my [brother] Edward's son,
    For that I was his father Edward's son,
    That blood already, like the pelican,
    [Hast thou] tapp'd out, and drunkenly carous'd .

2   My brother Gloucester, plain well-meaning soul,
    Whom fair befall in heaven 'mongst happy souls,
    May be a president and witness good
    That thou respect'st not spilling Edward's blood .

3   Join with the present sickness that I have,
    And thy unkindness be like crooked age,
    To crop at once a too-long withered flower.

4   Live in thy shame, but die not shame with thee!
    These words hereafter thy tormentors be !

5   Convey me to my bed, then to my grave ;
    Love they to live, that love and honor have .

Gaunt

1   Oh spare me not, my [brothers] Edwards sonne,
     For that I was his Father Edwards sonne :
     That blood already (like the Pellican)
     [Thou hast] tapt out, and drunkenly carows'd .

2   My brother Gloucester, plaine well meaning soule
     (Whom faire befall in heaven 'mongst happy soules)
     May be a president, and witnesse good,
     That thou respect'st not spilling Edwards blood :
     Joyne with the present sicknesse that I have,
     And thy unkindnesse be like crooked age,
     To crop at once a too-long wither'd flowre .

3   Live in thy shame, but dye not shame with thee,
     These words heereafter, thy tormentors bee .

4   Convey me to my bed, then to my grave,
     Love they to live, that love and honor have .

- not surprisingly, the opening attack on Richard, essentially calling him a blood-sucker, is passionate (4/5, F #1)

- the first four lines of F #2, blaming Richard (historically inaccurately) for Gaunt's brother's downfall, moves much more toward emotion (2/5)

- while Gaunt's three line onrushed ending of F #2, inviting Richard to kill him, becomes fully emotional (0/4); most modern texts reduce the lack of control that the onrush suggests by creating a new sentence (mt. #3) at this point

- and this emotion is sustained in Gaunt's final prophecy/curse that shame attach itself to Richard both in his life and after his death (0/3, F #3)

- and then, as noted in the introduction, comes the first unembellished lines in the speech, as the dying Gaunt leaves Richard with his last words passing a blessing onto the very antithesis of Richard, those 'that love and honor have'

The Life and Death of King Richard the Second
Yorke

Tut, tut, Grace me no Grace, nor Unckle me,
2.3.86–105

Background: Richard has seized all the assets of his cousin Bulling-brooke's deceased father, John of Gaunt, and, in Bullingbrooke's own words, declared his cousin 'A banisht Traytor'. While Richard is in Ireland, Bullingbrooke has returned to England, backed by a pow-erful rebel force. His uncle Yorke, still loyal to the current monarch Richard yet torn between Richard and Bullingbrooke has challenged Bullingbrooke to declare 'what pricks you on/to take advantage of the absent time,/And fright our Native Peace with selfe-borne Armes'. In an earlier scene Yorke has confessed 'Both are my kinsmen,/Th'one is my soveraigne, whom both my oath/And dutie bids defend: th'oth-er againe/Is my kinsman, whom the King hath wrong'd,/Whom conscience, and my kindred bids to right'. The first words out of Bullingbrooke's mouth are 'My noble Unckle' and 'My gracious Unckle', hence the following.

Style: one on one address in front of a larger group

Where: the countryside in Gloustershire

To Whom: his nephew Bullingbrooke, in front of Berkely, and Bullingbrooke's supporters including Northumberland, his son Hotspurre (here known as Harry Percie), Ross, and Willoughby

# of Lines: 19

Probable Timing: 1.00 minutes

York

1   Tut, tut !
    Grace me no grace, nor uncle me [no uncle] .

2   I am no traitor's uncle, and that word "grace"
    In an ungracious mouth, is but profane.

3   Why have [those] banish'd and forbidden legs
    Dar'd once to touch a dust of England's ground ?

4   But [then more] "why?"—why have they dar'd to march
    So many miles upon her peaceful bosom,
    Frighting her pale-fac'd villages with war
    And ostentation of despised arms ?

5   Com'st thou because th'anointed King is hence ?

6   Why, foolish boy, the King is left behind,
    And in my loyal bosom lies his power .

7   Were I but now [ ] Lord of such hot youth
    As when brave Gaunt, thy father, and myself
    Rescued the Black Prince, that young Mars of men,
    From forth the ranks of many thousand French,
    O then how quickly should this arm of mine,
    Now prisoner to the palsy, chastise thee,
    And minister correction to thy fault !

Yorke

1   Tut, tut, Grace me no Grace, nor Unckle me [ ],
    I am no Traytors Unckle ;and that word Grace,
    In an ungracious mouth, is but prophane .

2   Why have [these] banish'd, and forbidden Legges,
    Dar'd once to touch a Dust of Englands Ground ?

3   But [more then] why, why have they dar'd to march
    So many miles upon her peacefull Bosome,
    Frighting her pale-fac'd Villages with Warre,
    And ostentation of despised Armes ?

4   Com'st thou because th'anoynted King is hence ?

5   Why foolish Boy, the King is left behind,
    And in my loyall Bosome lyes his power .

6   Were I but now [the] Lord of such hot youth,
    As when brave Gaunt, thy Father, and my selfe
    Rescued the Black Prince, that yong Mars of men,
    From forth the Rankes of many thousand French :
    Oh then, how quickly should this Arme of mine,
    Now Prisoner to the Palsie, chastise thee,
    And minister correction to thy Fault .

Take Note: Though an obvious speech of rebuke based on a firm sense of mental control (30 capitals to 17 long spellings overall) F's first sentence and six extra breath thoughts show that Yorke is not at quite as much at ease at dealing with his rebellious nephew as modern texts suggest.

- the only (emotional) semicolon in the speech underscores Yorke's sense of honour, 'I am no Traytors Unckle;' , and the following surround phrase, the only one in the speech, unequivocally puts down his nephew for the in-part specious argument offered for his return, ' ; and that word Grace,/In an ungracious mouth, is but prophane . ' : that all this is in F #1 is a clear indication of Yorke's opening state of ill-ease

- however, most modern texts split F #1 in two by seeing the first line of reprimand as grammatically separate from the onrushed definitions of himself being in the right and his nephew in the wrong—ignoring the fact that this very onrush is a key to the struggle within him, of upholding the code of honour on the one hand yet feeling enormous sympathy for the nephew whom he believes has been legally wronged

- while the speech never develops into pure emotion, five of the six extra breath-thoughtss all seem to come before Yorke has something distasteful to add about his nephew's behaviour—see especially F #1-2

- while the speech ends in full intellectual control, as Yorke bluntly tells his nephew that were he young again he would have been quickly able to 'administer correction' to Bullingbrooke's current 'Fault' (12/4 in just seven lines of F #6), getting there involves a lot of passion, for every other sentence, save F #2's strong demand as to why the banished Bullingbrooke has returned (4/1) is strongly passionate (#1, 6/4; #3, 4/4; #4, 1/1; and #5, 2/3)

The Life and Death of King Richard the Second
Northumberland
The King of Heaven forbid our Lord the King
3.3.101–120

Background: before Northumberland can deliver Bullingbrooke's out-
wardly courteous and family oriented request, Richard, jumping to
reasonable conclusions both from events to date and the forces now
laid out before him, delivers a diatribe including 'Tell Bullingbrooke,
for yond me thinkes he is,/That every stride he makes upon my Land,/
Is dangerous treason'. Holding no illusions as to Bullingbrooke's true
ambitions, Richard continues 'But ere the Crowne he lookes for, live in
peace,/Ten thousand bloody crownes of Mothers Sonnes/Shall ill become the flower of Englands face'. The following is Northumberland's
very reasonable if, as events later prove, untruthful reply.

Style: one on one address in the open: the quarto suggests just to one
man on the walls above, the First Folio adds a small support group

Where: outside the castle near Harlech

To Whom: according to the quarto, Richard alone in front of the forces accompanying Northumberland: the Folio suggests that Richard
is accompanied by Bishop Carlile, Aumerle, Scroope, and Salisbury

# of Lines: 20

Probable Timing: 1.00 minutes

Northumberland

1 The King of heaven forbid our lord the King
  Should so with civil and uncivil arms
  Be rush'd upon !

2   Thy thrice-noble cousin,
  Harry Bullingbrook, doth humbly kiss thy hand,
  And by the honorable tomb he swears
  That stands upon your royal grandsire's bones,
  And by the royalties of both your bloods,
  (Currents that spring from one most gracious head)
  And by the buried hand of warlike Gaunt,
  And by the worth and honor of himself ,
  Comprising all that may be sworn or said,
  His coming hither hath no further scope
  [Than] for his lineal royalties, and to beg
  Enfranchisement immediate on his knees,
  Which on thy royal party granted once,
  His glittering arms he will commend to rust,
  His barbed steeds to stables, and his heart
  To faithful service of your Majesty .

3 This swears he, as he is a prince, [and] just,
  And as I am a gentleman I credit him .

Northumberland

1   The King of Heaven forbid our Lord the King
Should so with civill and uncivill Armes
Be rush'd upon : Thy thrice-noble Cousin,
Harry Bullingbrooke, doth humbly kisse thy hand,
And by the Honorable Tombe he sweares,
That stands upon your Royall Grandsires Bones,
And by the Royalties of both your Bloods,
(Currents that spring from one most gracious Head)
And by the buried Hand of Warlike Gaunt,
And by the Worth and Honor of himselfe,
Comprising all that may be sworne, or said,
His comming hither hath no further scope,
[Then] for his Lineall Royalties, and to begge
Infranchisement immediate on his knees :
Which on thy Royall partie graunted once,
His glittering Armes he will commend to Rust,
His barbed Steedes to Stables, and his heart
To faithfull service of your Majestie :
This sweares he, as he is a Prince, [is] just,
And as I am a Gentleman, I credit him .

Take Note: While the task of delivering the message to Richard should be simple enough, F's onrushed one sentence (in comparison to most modern texts' setting the opening denial of bad faith and closing reiteration of Bullingbrooke's honesty as separate sentences) suggests that Northumberland finds the task a little awkward, either through his own well–proven disapproval of Richard, or Richard's response to his arrival.

- the opening two and a half lines of denial, which modern texts hive off as mt. #1, plus the following eight line purple definition of Bullingbrooke's ancestry (shared with Richard through their 'Grandsire') as proof of honourable intent are highly intellectual (22/10 in eleven lines)

- but as he reaches the three lines explaining why Bullingbrooke comes thus armed (lines twelve-fourteen), Northumberland's mental discipline suddenly is joined if not subsumed by emotion (2/3), and the resultant passion even more pronounced during Northumberland's subsequent four line protestation that Bullingbrooke will disarm and swear 'faithfull service' once Richard grants a pardon (6/5), as it is in the final two and half line confirmation that Bullingbrooke is both a 'Prince' and a 'Gentleman' (2/1)

The First Part of King Henry the Fourth

King

My blood hath beene too cold and temperate,
between 1.3.1–21

Background: this is the opening speech of the second scene involving Henry. The 'indignities' referred to in line #2 are in part Hotspurre's refusal to hand over his prisoners (see next speech) for the customary royal right of disposal, and in part increased hostility from various noble houses (especially Worcester, Hotspurre's uncle), some of whom (Northumberland, Hotspurre's father) helped Henry depose Richard and thus become King.

Style: general address via one man to a larger group

Where: the palace

To Whom: Worcester, and his fellows somewhat hostile to Henry, Northumberland and his son Hotspurre, in front of Henry's supporters, including Sir Walter Blunt

# of Lines: 16

Probable Timing: 0.55 minutes

King

1   My blood hath been too cold and temperate,
      Unapt to stir at these indignities,
      And you have found me, for accordingly,
      You tread upon my patience ; but be sure,
      I will from henceforth rather be myself,
      Mighty and to be fear'd, [than] my condition,
      Which hath been smooth as oil, soft as young down,
      And therefore lost that title of respect
      Which the proud soul ne'er pays but to the proud .

---

2   {†}   I do see
      Danger and disobedience in thine eye .

3   O, sir, your presence is too bold and peremptory,
      And majesty might never yet endure
      The moody frontier of a servant brow.

4   You have good leave to leave us .

5   When we need
      Your use and counsel, we shall send for you .

King

1   My blood hath beene too cold and temperate,
    Unapt to stirre at these indignities,
    And you have found me ;x for accordingly,
    You tread upon my patience : But be sure,
    I will from henceforth rather be my Selfe,
    Mighty, and to be fear'd, [then] my condition
    Which hath beene smooth as Oyle, soft as yong Downe,
    And therefore lost that Title of respect,
    Which the proud soule ne're payes, but to the proud .

---

2   {†}   I do see
    Danger and disobedience in thine eye .

3   O sir, your presence is too bold and peremptory,
    And Majestie might never yet endure
    The moody Frontier of a servant brow,
    You have good leave to leave us .

4   When we need
    Your use and counsell, we shall send for you.

- the message in the only surround phrase of the speech should be sufficient warning for Worcester and his party to be careful

  " ; for accordingly,/You tread upon my patience : "

  especially when it is doubly weighted by being non-embellished and formed in part by the only (emotional) semicolon in the speech

- if this were not enough, the content of the totally non-embellished and relatively short (one and a half line) F #2

  "I do see /Danger and disobedience in thine eye . "

  clearly underscores all of Henry's current and future actions in the play towards his opponents: thus the remaining non-embellished line

  "You have good leave to leave us."

  should hardly come as a surprise (especially doubly weighted by being monosyllabic)

- while the speech opens emotionally (0/2 in the first two and a half lines of F #1), and is followed by the first (extra weighted, non-embellished) surround phrase already discussed

- the speech suddenly, and for the only time, turns to passion as Henry defines how he will be less forgiving to lack of 'respect' in the future (5/5 in the five and a half lines ending F #1)

- following this minor explosion, Henry regains an outward state of calm for the rest of the speech (just 2/1 in the six and a half lines of F #2-4), though the discussed non-embellished lines suggest that much is lurking beneath the outward calm

The First Part of King Henry the Fourth

King

Why yet [he] doth deny his Prisoners,
between 1.3.76–87

Background: Blunt seems to accept Hotspurre's explanation that he did not deny the prisoners as it stands, 'What ever Harry Percie then had said…May reasonably dye, and never rise/To do him wrong/…so he unsay it now'. However, Henry is not so easily swayed and goes straight to the heart of the problem.

Style: essentially an address via one man for the benefit of the larger group

Where: the palace

To Whom: Blunt, Henry's other supporters, the offending Hotspurre and his father Northumberland

# of Lines: 23

Probable Timing: 1.10 minutes

Take Note: Though sentence structures match, F's orthography shows that while Henry may begin by containing his emotions, he cannot keep them in check throughout.

King

1   Why, yet [he] doth deny his prisoners,
    But with proviso and exception,
    That we at our own charge shall ransom straight
    His brother-in-law, the foolish Mortimer,
    Who, [on] my soul, hath wilfully betray'd
    The lives of those that he did lead to fight
    Against [that] great magician, damn'd Glendower ,
    Whose daughter, as we hear, the Earl of March
    Hath lately married .

2   Shall our coffers then,
    Be emptied to redeem a traitor home ?

3   Shall we buy treason ? and indent with fears,
    When they have lost and forfeited themselves ?

4   No, on the barren [mountains] let him starve;
    For I shall never hold that man my friend
    Whose tongue shall ask me for one penny cost
    To ransom home revolted Mortimer .

---

5   Art thou not asham'd ?

6   {┼} Sirrah, henceforth
    Let me not hear you speak of Mortimer .

7   Send me your prisoners with the speediest means,
    Or you shall hear in such a kind from me
    As will displease [you] .

8   My Lord Northumberland,
    We license your departure with your son,
    Send us your prisoners, or [you will] hear of it .

King

1   Why yet [ ] doth deny his Prisoners,
     But with Proviso and Exception,
     That we at our owne charge, shall ransome straight
     His Brother-in-Law, the foolish Mortimer,
     Who ([in] my soule) hath wilfully betraid
     The lives of those, that he did lead to Fight,
     Against [the] great Magitian, damn'd Glendower :
     Whose daughter (as we heare) the Earle of March
     Hath lately married .

2   Shall our Coffers then,
     Be emptied, to redeeme a Traitor home ?

3   Shall we buy Treason ? and indent with Feares,
     When they have lost and forfeyted themselves .

4   No : on the barren [Mountaine] let him sterve :
     For I shall never hold that man my Friend,
     Whose tongue shall aske me for one peny cost
     To ransome home revolted Mortimer .

5   Art thou not asham'd ?

6   {†} Sirrah, henceforth
     Let me not heare you speake of Mortimer .

7   Send me your Prisoners with the speediest meanes,
     Or you shall heare in such a kinde from me
     As will displease [ye] .

8   My Lord Northumberland,
     We License your departure with your sonne,
     Send us your Prisoners, or [you'l] heare of it .

- no matter what else he says, Henry has two very fixed, irrevocable ideas about

    a. Hotspurre's and his family's seeking to ransom their kinsman who once had a legal claim to the throne: that Henry, regarding this as a threat, will have nothing to do with him is made clear by the surround phrases

    " . No : on the barren Mountaine let him sterve : "

    b. Hotspurre himself, expressed in the unembellished very short sentence F #5

    "Art thou not asham'd?"

- the opening remonstration of Hotspurre for the double act of denying his prisoners and making them a bargaining chip for his kinsman Mortimer's release is surprisingly mentally disciplined, emphasised by Henry's managing to do this without actually naming Hotspurre or talking directly to him (11/5, F #1): however, four of the five long spellings are attached to images of Mortimer (also referred to here by his other title, the 'Earle of March')

- Henry's refusal of any such transaction then becomes passionate (7/6, F #2-4)

- but as Henry directly confronts and dresses down Hotspurre (following the short unembellished F #5), emotions break through with the double command not to mention Mortimer again and to give over the Prisoners (2/5, F #6-7)

- while some control is re-established for the dismissal of Hotspurre's father (who is referred to by name) and Hotspurre (who is somewhat demeaningly referred to simply as Northumberland's 'sonne'), a little emotion still remains (4/2, F #8)

The First Part of King Henry the Fourth
Falstaff/Falstaffe

My Lord, {Falstaffe} I know ./But to say,
I know more harme in him...
between 2.4.464–480

Background: Falstaffe, supposedly playing the role of Hal, now replies to a diatribe from Hal, supposedly playing the role of his father, which. though it started out as a condemnation of Hal, ended up as an amazing attack on Falstaffe himself (foreshadowing perhaps the parting of the ways at the end of *The Second Part of King Henry the Fourth*). Whether Falstaffe maintains the supposed role of Hal throughout the following reply, or occasionally reverts to himself, is a choice for each production to decide. What triggers this speech is Hal's final tough-minded assessment of Falstaffe as 'That villanous abhominable mis-leader of Youth, Falstaffe, that old white-bearded Sathan'.

Style: starting as a one on one address in front of the larger group

Where: an Eastcheap tavern run by the Hostesse (sometimes known as Mistris Quickly)

To Whom: Hal, in front of Poines, Falstaffe's own men Gadshill, Peto, and Bardolph, the Hostesse, the Vintner, various servers, including Francis, and perhaps other tavern clientele

# of Lines: 16

Probable Timing: 0.55 minutes

Falstaff

1   My Lord, {[Falstaff]}I know .

---

2   But to say I know more harm in him [than] in
    myself , were to say more [than] I know .

3   That he is old
    (the more the pity) his white hairs do witness it,
    but that he is, saving your reverence, a whorema-
    ster, that I utterly deny .

4   If sack and sugar be a fault,
    [God] help the wicked !

5   If to be old and merry be a
    sin, then many an old host that I know is damn'd .

6   If to be fat be to be hated, then Pharaoh's lean kine are
    to be lov'd .

7   No, my good lord, banish Peto, banish
    Bardolph, banish [Poins], but for sweet Jacke [Falstaff],
    kind Jack [Falstaff], true Jack [Falstaff], valiant [Jack Fal-
    staff], and therefore more valiant, being as he is old Jack
    [Falstaff], banish not him thy Harry's company, banish
    not him thy Harry's company—banish plump Jack, and
    banish all the world .

Falstaffe

1 My Lord, {[Falstaffe]}I know .

---

2 But to say, I know more harme in him [then] in
   my selfe, were to say more [then] I know .

3   That hee is olde
   (the more the pittie) his white hayres doe witnesse it :
   but that hee is (saving your reverence) a Whore-master, that I utterly deny .

4   If Sacke and Sugar bee a fault,
   [Heaven] helpe the Wicked :if to be olde and merry, be a
   sinne, then many an olde Hoste that I know, is damn'd :
   if to be fat, be to be hated, then Pharaohs leane Kine are
   to be loved .

5   No, my good Lord, banish Peto, banish
   Bardolph, banish [Poines] : but for sweete Jacke [Falstaffe],
   kinde Jacke [Falstaff]e, true Jacke [Falstaffe], valiant [Jacke Fal-
   staffe], and therefore more valiant, being as hee is olde Jack
   [Falstaff]e,banish not him thy Harryes companie, banish
   not him thy Harryes companie ; banish plumpe Jacke, and
   banish all the World .

Take Note: It looks as if the vehemence of Hal-as-King's attack on him takes Falstaffe aback, for the opening short sentence (intellectual only, unusual for him except in special circumstances), and the extra breath-thought opening F #2 after 'But to say' (marked ,), suggest that it is not quite as easy to shrug off the attack as he would like.

- thus it's not surprising that though Falstaffe starts his reply wittily denying any harm in himself (F #2) and that while old he has never been a 'Whore-master' (F #3), the style is highly emotional (1/9)

- but as he warms to his task of self-defense, and in fine rhetorical style seeks to establish incontrovertible maxims about the worth of 'Sacke and Sugar' and of being 'olde and merry' and 'fat', he becomes very passionate (7/9, in the four lines of F #4), while the surround phrases opening and closing F #4 speak volumes to his beliefs and philosophy

- the rhetorical build seems far better served by the onrush as set in one sentence (F #4) rather than being split in three (mt. #4-6)

- and, now in full flow, appealing to the supposed king (i.e. Hal) to banish others while strenuously arguing for himself to be spared, so passion flows full and free (17/7 in just the six and a half lines of F #5), with the final surround phrase ending the speech both wonderfully heart-felt and incredibly ironic given the ending of their relationship when Hal eventually becomes king

The First Part of King Henry the Fourth
Glendower

My Daughter weepes, shee'le not part with you,
between 3.1.192–225

Background: with the rebels about to leave the safety of Wales, their Welsh host Glendower has brought in the wives of Hotspurre (Kate) and Mortimer (Glendower's own daughter). Since Glendower's daughter speaks no English and her husband Mortimer no Welsh, Glendower translates for her.

Style: on behalf of one person, to one person, as part of a six-handed scene

Where: in Wales, unspecified, but perhaps at the home of Glendower

To Whom: Mortimer, in front of Mortimer's wife, Hotspurre and Kate, and Worcester

# of Lines: 16

Probable Timing: 0.55 minutes

Take Note: Whether Glendower has the magical powers he claims or not, the surround phrases that make up F #4 suggest that he most certainly believes it, or at least talks the talk when necessary, for the impact of the major punctuation seems to stress the importance of what is being uttered as if it were a charm or spell.

Glendower

1   My daughter weeps, she'll not part with you,
    She'll be a soldier too, she'll to the wars.

2   She is desperate here, a peevish self-will'd harlotry,
    One that no persuasion can do good upon.

3   She bids you on the wanton rushes lay you down,
    And rest your gentle head upon her lap,
    And she will sing the song that pleaseth you,
    And on your eye-lids crown the god of sleep,
    Charming your blood with pleasing heaviness,
    Making such difference ['twixt] wake and sleep
    As is the difference betwixt day and night
    The hour before the heavenly- harness'd [team]
    Begins his golden progress in the east.

4   Do so,
    And those musicians that shall play to you
    Hang in the air a thousand leagues from [hence],
    And straight they shall be here.

5   Sit and attend.

Glendower

1   My Daughter weepes, shee'le not part with you,
    Shee'le be a Souldier too, shee'le to the Warres .

2   Shee is desperate heere : a peevish selfe-will'd Harlotry,
    One that no perswasion can doe good upon .

3   She bids you,
    On the wanton Rushes lay you downe,
    And rest your gentle Head upon her Lappe,
    And she will sing the Song that pleaseth you,
    And on your Eye-lids Crowne the God of Sleepe,
    Charming your blood with pleasing heavinesse ;x
    Making such difference [betwixt] Wake and Sleepe,
    As is the difference betwixt Day and Night,
    The houre before the Heavenly Harneis'd [Teeme]
    Begins his Golden Progresse in the East .

4   Doe so :
    And those Musitians that shall play to you,
    Hang in the Ayre a thousand Leagues from [thence] ;x
    And straight they shall be here : sit, and attend .

- whether Glendower's opening remarks are genuine, irritated, or amused, certainly his daughter's state of mind is of concern, as the first surround phrase suggests, ' . Shee is desperate heere : '

- and certainly the opening two sentences about her are very emotional (4/11 in just the four lines of F #1-2)

- the opening of F #3, as he translates into English his Welsh-only speaking daughter's remarks to her husband, is when his intellect begins to take over (8/5 in the five and a half lines to the semicolon), and as he describes the peaceful charm she intends to administer through her singing, so his mind assumes even more control (10/4 in the final four lines of F #3)

- F #4, his own charm to bring the airy 'Musitians' from afar.', has far more impact on him, and perhaps on his listeners as he speaks, than as set in the revamped mt. #4-5, for F #4's punctuation is far heavier (two colons and one semicolon plus two extra breath-thoughts, marked , , none of which are set in the modern texts) suggesting a mind working much harder to accomplish what it has set out to do: the fact that, as set, F #4 is a mixture of effort (lines 1 and 3) followed by non-embellishment (line 4) also suggest that the charm may be difficult to achieve, or so Glendower wants it to appear

The First Part of King Henry the Fourth
Falstaff/Falstaffe

Doe thou amend thy Face, and Ile amend thy Life:
between 3.3.24–48

Background: Bardolph has not been particularly sympathetic to Falstaffe's mood commenting 'Why, you are so fat, Sir John, that you must needes bee out of all compasse' which triggers the following verbal jabs at Bardolph's famous red nose. In *The Life of Henry the Fift*, Falstaffe's Boy remembers an earlier comment by his now deceased master about Bardolph's physiognomy, commenting 'Doe you not remember a saw Flea sticke upon Bardolph's Nose, and a said it was a blacke Soule burning in Hell'

Style: as part of a two-handed scene

Where: the tavern in Eastcheap

To Whom: Bardolph

# of Lines: 23

Probable Timing: 1.10 minutes

Falstaff

1   Do thou amend thy face, and I'll amend [my]
     life .

2   Thou art our admiral, thou bearest the lantern
     in the poop, but 'tis in the nose of thee .

3   Thou art the
     Knight of the burning Lamp .

---

4   No, I'll be sworn, I make as good use of it as
     many a man doth of a deaths-head or a memento mori .

5   I never see thy face but I think upon hell fire, and Dives
     that lived in purple ; for there he is in his robes, burning,
     burning .

6   If thou wert any way given to virtue, I would
     swear by thy face ; my oath should be "By this fire :
     [that's God's angel] ."

7   But thou art altogether given over, and wert indeed ,
     but for the light in thy face, the [son] of utter dark-
     ness .

8   When thou ran'st up Gads hill in the night to
     catch my horse, if I did not think [ ] thou hadst been
     an ignis fatuus or a ball of wildfire, there's no purchase
     in money .

9   O, thou art a perpetual triumph, an ever-
     lasting bonfire light !

10   Thou hast sav'd me a thousand
     marks in links and torches, walking with thee in the
     night betwixt tavern and tavern; but the sack that
     thou hast drunk me would have bought me lights as
     good cheap [at] the dearest chandler's in Europe .

11   I have
     maintain'd that salamander of yours with fire any time
     this two and thirty years, [God] reward me for it !

Falstaffe

1   Doe thou amend thy Face, and Ile amend [thy]
Life : Thou art our Admirall, thou bearest the Lanterne
in the Poope, but 'tis in the Nose of thee ; thou art the
Knight of the burning Lampe .

---

2   No, Ile be sworne : I make as good use of it, as
many a man doth of a Deaths-Head, or a Memento Mori .

3   I never see thy Face, but I thinke upon Hell fire, and Dives
that lived in Purple ; for there he is in his Robes burning,
burning .

4   If thou wert any way given to vertue, I would
sweare by thy Face ; my Oath should bee, By this Fire : [ ]
But thou art altogether given over ; and wert indeede,
but for the Light in thy Face, the [Sunne] of utter Darkenesse .

5   When thou ran'st up Gads-Hill in the Night, to
catch my Horse, if I did not thinke [that] thou hadst beene
an Ignis fatuus, or a Ball of Wild-fire, there's no Purchase
in Money .

6   O, thou art a perpetuall Triumph, an ever-
lasting Bone-fire-Light : thou hast saved me a thousand
Markes in Linkes and Torches, walking with thee in the
Night betwixt Taverne and Taverne : But the Sack that
thou hast drunke me, would have bought me Lights as
good cheape, [as] the dearest Chandlers in Europe .

7   I have
maintain'd that Salamander of yours with fire, any time
this two and thirtie yeeres, [Heaven] reward me for it .

- Though the attack on Bardolph contains some splendid invective, the fact that at no time in this passionate yet intellectually based speech (51/22 in just twenty-three lines) does Falstaffe resort to pure emotion suggests that at base he is not too serious.Whether mocking or semi-serious, Falstaffe has some very barbed moments, as the surround phrases show

  " . Doe thou amend thy Face, and Ile amend thy Life : Thou art our Admirall, thou bearest the Lanterne in the Poope, but 'tis in the Nose of thee ; thou art the Knight of the burning Lampe . "

  " . No, Ile be sworne : "

  "If thou wert any way given to vertue, I would sweare by thy Face ; my Oath should bee, By this Fire : [ ] But thou art altogether given over ; and wert indeede, but for the Lightin thy Face, the [Sunne] of utter Darkenesse . "

  especially with so many of them being partially formed by the (emotional) semicolon

- thus the opening attack on Bardolph's face starts out passionately (8/5) and as an onrush, perhaps suggesting Falstaffe is not in as much control as he would like to be (or not holding himself back)—an onrush spoiled by most modern texts that split F #1 into three

- and then his mind takes full charge, reveling in comparing Bardolph's face to a 'Deaths-Head' (F #2) and (F #3) a reminder of 'Hell fire' (9/2)

- emotion creeps in a little via long spellings and semicolons as he puns on Bardolph being a 'Sunne' of 'Darknesse' (9/5, F #4), while the recounting of Bardolph's nose as a guiding light at Gads-Hill releases his mental powers once more (9/2, F #5)

- while the final triumphant balancing off of the money saved in torches against the cost of drink is wonderfully passionate (16/9, F #6-7)

The First Part of King Henry the Fourth

Worcester

O no, my Nephew must not know, Sir Richard,
between 5.2.1–40

Background: despite Henry's dismissal of Worcester's arguments, he has offered a pardon to all, 'And will they take the offer of our Grace:/Both he, and they, and you; yea every man/Shall be my friend againe, and Ile be his', threatening 'Rebuke and dread correction' if such yielding is not forthcoming. Here Worcester explains to Vernon why Hotspurre should not be told of the King's offer.

Style: as part of a two-handed scene

Where: close to the rebel's camp

To Whom: a (younger) fellow rebel leader, Sir Richard Vernon

# of Lines: 28

Probable Timing: 1.25 minutes

Take Note: Though overall the speech seems quite passionate (22/23), F's orthography reveals Worcester's mind establishing a thought intellectually or passionately, and then, in developing it in full, becoming emotional.

Worcester

1 O no, my nephew must not know, Sir Richard,
   The liberal [and] kind offer of the King .

2 It is not possible, it cannot be,
   The King [should] keep his word in loving us.

3 He will suspect us still, and find a time
   To punish this offense in [other] faults .

4 Supposition all our lives shall be stuck full of eyes,
   For treason is but trusted like the fox,
   Who [never] so tame, so cherish'd and lock'd up,
   Will have a wild trick of his ancestors .

5 Look how [we] can, or sad or merrily,
   Interpretation will misquote our looks,
   And we shall feed like oxen at a stall,
   The better cherish'd, still the nearer death .

6 My nephew's trespass may be well forgot,
   It hath the excuse of youth, and heat of blood,
   And an adopted name of privilege,
   A hair-brain'd Hotspur, govern'd by a spleen .

7 All his offenses live upon my head,
   And on his father's .

8   We did train him on,
   And his corruption being ta'en from us,
   We as the spring of all shall pay for all .

9 Therefore, good cousin, let not Harry know,
   In any case, the offer of the King .

Enter Hotspurre

10 The King will bid you battle presently .

11 There is no seeming mercy in the King .

12 He calls us rebels, traitors, and will scourge
    With haughty arms this hateful name in us .

Worcester

1   O no, my Nephew must not know, Sir Richard,
    The liberall [ ] kinde offer of the King .

2   It is not possible, it cannot be,
    The King [would] keepe his word in loving us,
    He will suspect us still, and finde a time
    To punish this offence in [others] faults :
    Supposition, all our lives, shall be stucke full of eyes ;x
    For Treason is but trusted like the Foxe,
    Who [ne're] so tame, so cherisht, and lock'd up,
    Will have a wilde tricke of his Ancestors :
    Looke how [he] can, or sad or merrily,
    Interpretation will misquote our lookes,
    And we shall feede like Oxen at a stall,
    The better cherisht, still the nearer death .

3   My Nephewes trespasse may be well forgot,
    It hath the excuse of youth, and heate of blood,
    And an adopted name of Priviledge,
    A haire-brain'd Hotspurre, govern'd by a Spleene :
    All his offences live upon my head,
    And on his Fathers .

4   We did traine him on,
    And his corruption being tane from us,
    We as the Spring of all, shall pay for all :
    Therefore good Cousin, let not Harry know
    In any case, the offer of the King .

               Enter Hotspurre

5   The King will bid you battell presently .

6   There is no seeming mercy in the King .

7   He cals us Rebels, Traitors, and will scourge
    With haughty armes, this hatefull name in us .

- thus, the first line of F #1 is intellectual as he sets up the facts (3/0), the second more emotional as he explains why (1/2)

- modern texts tend to regard the following elaboration of why Hotspurre must not be told of the King's apparent generous offer of peace as far more intellectually controlled than F's orthography and especially sentence structure have set it out—for most modern texts divide F's long onrushed sentence #2 into no fewer than four logical, grammatically correct sentences, ignoring that the enormity of what Worcester is suggesting plus the short time he has before Hotspurre joins them may be wreaking havoc on normal rhetorical/syntactical niceties

- not surprisingly, the first eight lines of F #2, establishing the theory as to why the King would not trust them, are passionate (4/6), the concluding four lines, explaining that no matter how the king will seem to behave they are still doomed, become emotional (1/3)

- for some reason modern texts also divide F #3's onrush in two, thus obscuring the potential strain of Worcester's true reason for refusing the King's offer—that while Hotspurre's 'trespasse' may be forgiven as that of a young man, Worcester's and Hotspurre's father's will not, at the cost of their lives

- with the elaboration coming first, F #3 starts out passionate as Hotspurre's possible forgiveness is explored (4/7 in the first four lines)

- while the summary as to the fate of the older characters is intellectually handled (5/1, the last line and a half of F #3 and all of F #4)

- however, once Hotspurre enters, Worcester's first two short sentences (F #5-6) suggest that while there may be passion in passing on the information (4/3, including F #7), he is taking great care to make the news so absolute that Hotspurre will not dispute the facts, the capitalised words in F #7 ('Rebels' and 'Traitors') giving no quarter for challenge or debate

The First Part of King Henry the Fourth
Falstaff/Falstaffe

Imbowell'd ? If thou imbowell mee to day, Ile
5.4.111–129

Background: following his farewell words to Hotspurre whom he has killed in single combat Hal has discovered Falstaffe lying prone on the ground, apparently dead. Not realising that Falstaffe is in fact conscious, and has been 'playing dead' to avoid any chance of harm in a brief battle-field encounter with Dowglas, the ferocious Scottish rebel, Hal makes his farewells to Falstaffe too. However, there is the possibility that the penultimate line 'Imbowell'd will I see thee by and by' is said because Hal has suddenly realised that Falstaffe has been faking things for quite a while, and really is alive. Certainly the suggestion of 'embowelling' triggers a very definite negative response in Falstaffe, as this speech clearly shows.

Style: solo

Where: on the battlefield, alongside the body of the just killed Harry Percy also known as Hotspurre

To Whom: solo and audience address

# of Lines: 17

Probable Timing: 0.55 minutes

Falstaff

Falstaffe riseth up

1 Embowell'd ! if thou embowel me to-day, I'll
give you leave to powder me and eat me too to-morrow .

2 [S'blood],'twas time to counterfeit, or that hot termagant
Scot had paid me scot and lot too .

3   Counterfeit ?

4   [I lie,] I am no counterfeit .

5   To die is to be a counterfeit, for he is but the
counterfeit of a man, who hath not the life of a man ; but
to counterfeit dying, when a man thereby liveth, is to be
no counterfeit, but the true and perfect image of life indeed .

6   The better part of valour is discretion, in the
which better part I have saved my life .

7   ['Zounds] I am afraid of
this gun-powder Percy though he be dead .

8   How if he
should counterfeit too and rise ?

9   [By my faith], I am afraid he would
prove the better counterfeit .

10   Therefore I'll make him sure,
yea, and I'll swear I kill'd him .

11   Why may not he rise as
well as I?

12   Nothing confutes me but eyes, and [nobody]
sees me .

13   Therefore, sirrah, with a new wound in your thigh,
come you along [with] me .

Falstaffe

Falstaffe riseth up

1   Imbowell'd ?

2   If thou imbowell mee to day, Ile
give you leave to powder me, and eat me too to morow .

3   [ ] 'Twas time to counterfet, or that hotte Termagant Scot,
had paid me scot and lot too .

4   Counterfeit ?

5   [ ] I am no counterfeit ; to dye, is to be a counterfeit, for hee is but the
counterfeit of a man, who hath not the life of a man : But
to counterfeit dying, when a man thereby liveth, is to be
no counterfeit, but the true and perfect image of life indeede .

6   The better part of Valour, is Discretion ;x in the
which better part, I have saved my life .

7   [ ] I am affraide of
this Gun-powder Percy though he be dead .

8   How if hee
should counterfeit too, and rise ?

9   [ ] I am afraid hee would
prove the better counterfeit: therefore Ile make him sure :
yea, and Ile sweare I kill'd him .

10   Why may not hee rise as
well as I : Nothing confutes me but eyes, and no-bodie
sees me .

11   Therefore sirra, with a new wound in your thigh
come you along [ ] me .

Take Note: F's orthography in this speech is not as fulsome as most of Falstaffe's earlier ones, for throughout F #1-5 there are ten non-embellished phrases compared to just six with some sort of release—perhaps suggesting that at times his near-death-by-sword encounter with Dowglas (and later the emotion released vis-à-vis the possibility of Hotspurre not being dead) really does get to him.

- his reaction to the possibility of being 'imbowell'd' (i.e. disembow-eled and stuffed) is much more marked as a separate sentence (F #1) than being treated as the start of a longer sentence as most modern texts set

- similarly, the need to correct his own Freudian slip as to how he es-caped death-by-Dowglas (through 'Counterfeit') is more interesting as the longer sentence F #5 than the two part mt. #4-5: F's chop logic being tacked on via an (emotional) semicolon, suggests that Falstaffe may be working harder than his modern counterpart to recover face for himself and the audience

- it is only when he finally manages to justify his actions, via the max-im of F #6, that intellect momentarily peeps through (2/1)

- the variations in dealing with the dead Hotspurre (here referred to by the family name of 'Percy') sets up some interesting possibilities, for while Falstaffe's opening recognition of his own fear is again slightly intellectual (2/1, F #7), it is quickly followed by an emotional detail-ing of why he is afraid and how he plans to deal with it and turn it to his own advantage (1/4, F #9-10)

- and the non-embellished finish (F #11) offers several possibilities—that he is staying quiet so no-one can overhear; or concentrating on exactly where to make the thigh-wound; or even being quiet in case, against all the odds, Hotspurre is still alive

The Second Part of King Henry the Fourth
Pistoll

I tell thee what, Corporall Bardolph, I...
between 2.4.153–183

Background: in response to Dol's verbal attack Pistoll has already threatened 'God let me not live, but I will murther your Ruffe, for this'. The following is his continued rant. One note; the 'Sweetheart' in F #10's last line is a reference to his sword.

Style: initially to one person, and then in general to all in the group

Where: an Eastcheap tavern

To Whom: initially Bardolfe, in front of Falstaffe, Dol, the Hostesse, Falstaffe's Page, and perhaps the Drawer

# of Lines: 18

Probable Timing: 1.00 minutes

Take Note: The problem of whether Pistoll speaks prose, as F sets, or verse, as set by many modern texts that rework the quarto text, is always open to discussion. In this case modern texts have gone one stage further and set verse without any quarto authority, for here quarto and F set the passage in prose. Whether verse or prose, F's mixture of surround phrases, short sentences, outrageous classical references, and excessive orthography (65 different releases in just eighteen lines) suggests a character lost in the throes of self aggrandizement and braggadocio.

Pistoll

1   I tell thee what, Corporal Bardolph, I
     could tear her .

2   I'll be reveng'd [of] her .

---

3   I'll see her damn'd first, to Pluto's damn'd lake, [by this
     hand], to [th'infernal] deep, with Erebus and
     Tortures vile also .

4   Hold hook and line, say I .

5   Down : down
     dogs! down [fators]! have we not Hiren here ?

---

6   These be good humors indeed !

7   Shall pack-horses
     And hollow pamper'd jades of Asia,
     Which cannot go but thirty [mile a] day,/
     Compare with [Cæsars] and with Cannibals
     And [Troiant] Greeks ?

8   Nay, rather damn them with
     King Cerberus,/and let the welkin roar .

9   Shall we fall foul for toys?

---

10   Die men, like dogs ! give crowns like pins ! have
     we not Hiren here ?

---

11   Then feed and be fat, my fair Calipolis .

12   Come, [give's] some sack .

13   Si fortune me tormente, sperato me [contento] .

---

14   Fear we broadsides ? no, let the fiend give fire :
     Give me some sack, and sweet heart, lie thou there{.}

Pistoll

1   I tell thee what, Corporall Bardolph, I
could teare her : Ile be reveng'd [on] her .

2   Ile see her damn'd first : to Pluto's damn'd Lake, [ ]
to [the Infernall] Deepe, where Erebus and Tortures vilde
also .

3   Hold Hooke and Line, say I : Downe : downe
Dogges, downe [Fates] : have wee not Hiren here ?

4   These be good Humors indeede .

5   Shall Pack-
Horses, and hollow-pamper'd Jades of Asia, which cannot goe but thirtie [miles] day, compare with [Cæsar], and
with Caniballs, and [Trojan] Greekes ? nay, rather damne
them with King Cerberus, and let the Welkin roare :/ shall
wee fall foule for Toyes ?

6   Die men, like Dogges ; give Crownes like Pinnes :
Have we not Hiren here ?

7   Then feed, and be fat (my faire Calipolis .)

8   Come, [give
me] some Sack, Si fortune me tormente, sperato me [con-
tente] .

9   Feare wee broad-sides ?

10   No, let the Fiend give fire :
Give me some Sack : and Sweet-heart lye thou there {.}

- the surround phrases underscore several strands

  a. Pistoll's anger at Dol's refusal, ' : Ile be reveng'd on her . ', plus ' . Ile see her damn'd first : '

  b. and by extension his fury with everyone ' : shal wee fall foule for Toyes ? ' and ' . Hold Hooke and Line, say I : Downe : downe Dogges, downe Fates : have wee not Hiren here ? '

  c. to defiance of the devil provided Pistoll can get enough drink,

  " . No, let the Fiend give fire : Give me some Sack : and Sweet -heart lye thou there {.} "

- with such a 'Swaggerer' (to use the Hostesse's derogatory description of him, speech # 25 above) it's not surprising that this classical-reference laden (often incorrectly) rant should be passionate throughout, with intellect slightly dominating emotion (37/28 overall)

- where intellect dominates is obviously in the two passages of classical references (F #2, 6/3, and the first three lines of F #5—to the question mark—8/2) and in the somewhat incorrect Italian in F #8 (attempting to quote the maxim, 'If fortune torments me, hope contents me.')

- the only emotional moment is the challenge to the world at large in F #9's 'Feare wee broad-sides?' (0/2)

The Second Part of King Henry the Fourth

King

How many thousand of my poorest Subjects
3.1.4–31

Background: the King is alone, awaiting the arrival of his key advisors Warwicke and Surrey for a war council. As with several Shakespeare characters in crisis (Brutus, Macbeth, and even his own son in *The Life of Henry the Fift*) Henry is finding, to his obvious discomfort, sleep is eluding him. The following is his first speech in the play.

Style: solo

Where: the palace

To Whom: the (abstract) idea of sleep and (perhaps) the offstage audience

# of Lines: 28

Probable Timing: 1.20 minutes

Take Note: With lack of sleep being one of the key Shakespearean indicators that there is deep perturbation in the character's soul, it's not surprising to find twelve extra breath thoughts in the speech. What is fascinating is that they essentially cluster in just two spots. Surprisingly, despite such deep self-examination, Henry's intellect is not swamped emotionally (45/32 overall), save for the opening and closing sentences of the speech .

King

1　How many thousand of my poorest subjects
　Are at this hour asleep!

2　　　　　　　　　O sleep! O gentle sleep!
　Nature's soft nurse, how have I frighted thee,
　That thou no more wilt weigh my eye-lids down,
　And steep my senses in forgetfulness?

3　Why rather, sleep, liest thou in smoky cribs,
　Upon uneasy [pallets] stretching thee,
　And hush'd with buzzing night-flies to thy slumber,
　[Than] in the perfum'd chambers of the great,
　Under the canopies of costly state,
　And lull'd with [sound] of sweetest melody ?

4　O thou dull god, why li'st thou with the vile
　In loathsome beds, and leav'st the kingly couch
　A watch-case or a common 'larum-bell ?

5　Wilt thou upon the high and giddy mast
　Seal up the ship-boys eyes, and rock his brains
　In cradle of the rude imperious surge,
　And in the visitation of the winds,
　Who take the ruffian billows by the top,
　Curling their monstrous heads and hanging them
　With deaf'ning [clamor] in the slippery clouds,
　That with the hurly death itself awakes ?

6　Canst thou, O partial sleep, give [then] repose
　To the wet sea-boy in an hour so rude,
　And in the calmest and most stillest night,
　With all appliances and means to boot,
　Deny it to a king ?

7　　　　　　　　　Then happy low, lie down !

8　Uneasy lies the head that wears a crown .

King

1   How many thousand of my poorest Subjects
     Are at this howre asleepe ?

2   O Sleepe, O gentle Sleepe,
     Natures soft Nurse, how have I frighted thee,
     That thou no more wilt weigh my eye-lids downe,
     And steepe my Sences in Forgetfulnesse ?

3   Why rather (Sleepe) lyest thou in smoakie Cribs,
     Upon uneasie [Pallads] stretching thee,
     And huisht with bussing Night, flyes to thy slumber,
     [Then] in the perfum'd Chambers of the Great ?
     Under the Canopies of costly State,
     And lull'd with [sounds] of sweetest Melodie ?

4   O thou dull God, why lyest thou with the vilde,
     In loathsome Beds, and leav'st the Kingly Couch,
     A Watch-case, or a common Larum-Bell ?

5   Wilt thou, upon the high and giddie Mast,
     Seale up the Ship-boyes Eyes, and rock his Braines,
     In Cradle of the rude imperious Surge,
     And in the visitation of the Windes,
     Who take the Ruffian Billowes by the top,
     Curling their monstrous heads, and hanging them
     With deaff'ning [Clamors] in the slipp'ry Clouds,
     That with the hurley, Death it selfe awakes ?

6   Canst thou (O partiall Sleepe) give [thy] Repose
     To the wet Sea-Boy, in an houre so rude :
     And in the calmest, and most stillest Night,
     With all appliances, and meanes to boote,
     Deny it to a King ?

7   Then happy Lowe, lye downe,
     Uneasie lyes the Head, that weares a Crowne .

- the key concern for Henry is expressed emotionally in the last two words of the opening sentence—essentially asking why he cannot, like his 'Subjects', be at this 'howre asleepe?'

- and then, as he starts to address 'Sleepe' directly, passion floods in as he envisages sleep for the ordinary man (4/4 in the first three lines of F #3)

- Henry then re-establishes firm intellectual control as he asks why it cannot lie in the 'perfum'd Chambers of the Great?' but instead goes to 'loathsome Beds' and leaves him awake as if he were the first line of defence. 'A watch-' ready to ring the 'Larum-Bell' (12/2, in just six lines, the three ending F #3 and all of F #4)

- and as he voices the 'Larum-Bell' idea, he needs three extra breaths in this sentence—and three more in the two lines of the next sentence (F #5)—to maintain his intellectual discipline

- the need for extra breaths continues at the start of F #5 as he imagines (envies?) 'Ship-Boyes' in the most dangerous and uncomfortable spot (the 'high and giddie-Mast') being able to sleep through noise that would awaken 'Death' itself, and his emotions rise to meet his intellect (19/13 in the twelve and a half lines of F #5-6)

- in finishing this passionate passage, as he finds himself in comparison to the 'wet Sea-Boy' unable to sleep in the 'most stillest Night', four extra breaths make themselves felt—in the last line of F #5 and in lines 2-5 of F #6

- thus it's not surprising that the speech ends on a high emotional note, with, according to most modern texts, an onrushed sentence accepting that the 'Lowe' can sleep while 'Uneasie' he cannot, (3/6 in just the one and a half lines of F #7)

The Second Part of King Henry the Fourth
Shallow

I was once of Clements Inne ; where (I thinke) they will
between 3.2.14–38

Background: Shallow is a rich land owner and Justice of the Peace liv-
ing in the tranquility of the Gloucestershire countryside. The following is a collage of his smaller opening speeches, setting up both
his extreme loquaciousness and his tendency to embellish upon the
truth more than somewhat. One note; the 'Bona-Roba's' referred
to in sentence #3 is a polite reference to prostitutes.

Style: as part of a two-handed scene

Where: in front of Shallow's home, or in his gardens

To Whom: his cousin Silence, another Justice of the Peace

# of Lines: 19

Probable Timing: 1.00 minutes

Take Note: F offers a delightful short-hand method of representing old
age with vocal styles quickly shifting to match Shallow's jumping
from topic to topic, sometimes past sometimes present, as well as
highly onrushed sentences, the latter hardly ever set by modern texts.

Shallow

1 I was once of Clement's Inn, where I think they will
talk of mad Shallow yet .

2 [By the mass], I was call'd any thing, and I would have done
any thing indeed too, and roundly too .

3   There was I, and
little John Doit of Staffordshire, and black George [Barnes],
and Francis [Pickbone], and Will Squele, a [Cotsole] man .

4   You
had not four such swinge bucklers in all the Inns [a]
Court again; and I may say to you, we knew where
the bona-robas were and had the best of them all at
commandment .

5   Then was Jack Falstaff, now Sir John,
a boy, and page to Thomas Mowbray, Duke of Nor-
folk .

6   The same Sir John, the very same .

7   I [see] him
break [Scoggin's] head at the court-gate, when[a] was
a crack not thus high ; and the very same day did I fight
with one [Samson] Stockfish, a fruiterer, behind [Gray's
Inn] .

8   [Jesu, Jesu,] the mad days that I have spent !

9   And to see
how many of mine old acquaintance are dead !

10 Certain, 'tis certain, very sure, very sure .

11 Death, [as the Psalmist saith], is certain to all, all shall die .

Shallow

1   I was once of Clements Inne ;where (I thinke) they will
     talke of mad Shallow yet .

2   [ ] I was call'd any thing : and I would have done
     any thing indeede too, and roundly too .

3   There was I, and
     little John Doit of Staffordshire, and blacke George [Bare],
     and Francis Pick-bone, and Will Squele, a Cot-sal-man, you
     had not foure such Swindge-bucklers in all the Innes [of]
     Court againe : And I may say to you, wee knew where
     the Bona-Roba's were, and had the best of them all at
     commandement .

4   Then was Jacke Falstaffe (now Sir John)
     a Boy, and Page to Thomas Mowbray, Duke of Nor-
     folke .

5   The same Sir John, the very same : I [saw] him
     breake [Scoggan's] Head at the Court-Gate, when [hee]was
     a Crack, not thus high : and the very same day did I fight
     with one [Sampson] Stock-fish, a Fruiterer, behinde [Greyes-
     Inne] .

6   [Oh] the mad dayes that I have spent ! and to see
     how many of mine olde Acquaintance are dead ?

7   Certaine : 'tis certaine : very sure, very sure :
     Death [ ] is certaine to all, all shall dye .

- Shallow's continuing to establish himself as a man to be reckoned with, including celebrating a lurid past, are all beautifully highlighted in the surround phrases

  " . I was once of Clements Inne ; where (I thinke) they will talke of mad Shallow yet . I was call'd any thing : and I would have done any thing indeede too, and roundly too . "

  as are recollections of supposedly powerful friends

  " . The same Sir John, the very same : "

  and the ability to pass on pearls of wisdom

  " . Certaine : 'tis certaine : very sure, very sure : Death is certaine to all, all shall dye . "

- the opening of the speech, enhanced by the semicolon and made up of surround phrases is wondrously passionate (3/3 in the one and a half lines of F #1), followed by an immediate switch to intimacy as he recollects how he was (would like to have been?) known (0/1, F #2)

- and then the onrush starts, with the intellectual naming of his friends (10/1, the first two and half lines of F #3), immediately followed by a passionate recollection of their swashbuckling and whore-hunting days (6/7, the final three and half lines of F #3)

- the recalling of Falstaffe is wonderfully intellectual (22/7, in the six and a half lines of F #4 and the onrushed #5

- while the final celebration of self (F #6) and the quick shift into acknowledging death (F #7) become highly emotional (1/6 in the last four lines)

The Second Part of King Henry the Fourth
Falstaff/Falstaffe

Is the old King dead ?
between 5.3.120–138

Background: in the middle of the festivities, Pistoll, another of Falstaffe's cronies, arrives with news that Falstaffe has been longing for, word of the old King's death and that with the accession of Hal, 'Sir John, thy tender Lambe-kinne, now is King'.

Style: the group as a whole, and individual members therein

Where:

in front of Shallow's home, or in his gardens

To Whom: the group as a whole, including Shallow, Silence, Davey, Pistoll, Bardolfe, and Falstaffe's Page

# of Lines: 15

Probable Timing: 0.50 minutes

Take Note: Most modern texts follow the quarto and set the (shaded) opening to this speech in prose. However, F seems to underscore Falstaffe's joy by setting irregular verse until the need for practicality takes over.

Falstaff

1   {†} Is the old king dead ?

2   Away [Bardolph] ! saddle my horse .

3   Master Robert Shallow,
     choose what office thou wilt in the land, 'tis thine .

4   Pistol,
     I will double charge thee with dignities .

5   Carry Master Silence to bed .

6   Master Shallow, my
     Lord Shallow—be what thou wilt, I am Fortune's steward—
     get on thy boots .

7   We'll ride all night .

8   O sweet Pistol !

9   Away, Bardolph !

10   Come Pistol, utter more to me, and
     withal devise something to do thyself good .

11   Boot,
     boot, Master Shallow !

12   I know the young king is sick for
     me .

13   Let us take any man's horses, the laws of Eng-
     land are at my commandement .

14   [Blessed] are they [that]
     have been my friends, and woe [to] my Lord Chief
     Justice !

Falstaffe

1 {†} Is the old King dead ?

---

2 Away [Bardolfe], Sadle my Horse,
Master Robert Shallow, choose what Office thou wilt
In the Land, 'tis thine .

3   Pistol, I will double charge thee
With Dignities .

---

4 Carrie Master Silence to bed : Master Shallow, my
Lord Shallow, be what thou wilt, I am Fortunes Steward .

5 Get on thy Boots, wee'l ride all night .

6   Oh sweet Pistoll :
Away Bardolfe : Come Pistoll, utter more to mee : and
withall devise something to do thy selfe good .

7   Boote,
boote Master Shallow, I know the young King is sick for
mee .

8   Let us take any mans Horsses : The Lawes of England are at my command'ment .

9   [Happie] are they, [which]
have beene my Friendes : and woe [unto] my Lord Chiefe
Justice .

- amazingly, there's not a scrap of wasted emotion in Falstaffe's irregular verse opening: it's as if his mind has hit overdrive and is busily planning all the moves that need to be made at one and the same time (17/0 in the six and a half lines of F #1-3, the verse, and the first prose sentence , F #4)

- from then on the rest of the speech becomes one long release of intellect and emotion as the passion and surround phrases flow (16/14 in the eight and a bit lines ending the speech)

- and while the early surround phrases are either commands (the opening of F #4 and the second instruction of F #6), or requests for corroboration (the remainder of F #6, save for the last phrase), those that make up the last two sentences of the speech would be enough to cause the ghost of Hal's father to roll over in his grave, and the still alive Chiefe Justice to fear for his life

> " . Let us take any mans Horsses : The Lawes of England are at
> my command'ment . Happie are they, which have beene my
> Friendes : and woe unto my Lord Chiefe Justice . "

The Life of Henry the Fift
Bishop of Canterbury

My Lord, Ile tell you, that selfe Bill is urg'd,
between 1.1.1–81

Background: the character's first speech of the play, in which he explains that he is planning to urge and offer the Church's financial support for a war in France—so as to protect the Church from an even greater anticipated peace-time loss.

Style: as part of a two-handed scene

Where: an anteroom of the palace

To Whom: Bishop of Ely

# of Lines: 26

Probable Timing: 1.20 minutes

Take Note: F's orthography makes it very clear that after a careful opening, the Bishop almost loses self-control, for he cannot free himself from listing every tiny detail of how much the Church will lose financially if the current bill goes through—and that it's only his final offer to King Henry that might save the situation.

Bishop of Canterbury

1   My Lord, I'll tell you, that self bill is urg'd
     Which in th'eleventh year of [the] last king's reign
     Was like, and had indeed against us pass'd,
     But that the scambling and unquiet time
     Did push it out of farther question .

---

2   It must be thought on .
3   If it pass against us,
     We lose the better half of our possession ;
     For all the temporal lands, which men devout
     By testament have given to the Church,
     Would they strip from us ; being valu'd thus :
     As much as would maintain, to the King's honor,
     Full fifteen earls and fifteen hundred knights,
     Six thousand and two hundred good esquires ;
     And to relief of lazars, and weak age
     Of indigent faint souls past corporal toil,
     A hundred almshouses right well supplied;
     And to the coffers of the king beside,
     A thousand pounds by th'year .
4   Thus runs the bill .

---

5   {†} For mitigation of this bill,

     {†}   I have made an offer to his Majesty,
     Upon our spiritual convocation,
     And in regard of causes now in hand,
     Which I have open'd to his Grace at large,
     As touching France, to give a greater sum
     [Than] ever at one time the clergy yet
     Did to his predecessors part withal.

Bishop of Canterbury

1   My Lord, Ile tell you, that selfe Bill is urg'd,
Which in th'eleventh yere of [ÿ] last Kings reign
Was like, and had indeed against us past,
But that the scambling and unquiet time
Did push it out of farther question .

2   It must be thought on : if it passe against us,
We loose the better halfe of our Possession :
For all the Temporall Lands, which men devout
By Testament have given to the Church,
Would they strip from us ; being valu'd thus,
As much as would maintaine, to the Kings honor,
Full fifteene Earles, and fifteene hundred Knights,
Six thousand and two hundred good Esquires :
And to reliefe of Lazars, and weake age
Of indigent faint Soules, past corporall toyle,
A hundred Almes-houses, right well supply'd :
And to the Coffers of the King beside,
A thousand pounds by th'yeere .

3   Thus runs the Bill .

4   {t} For mittigation of this Bill,

    {t}   I have made an offer to his Majestie,
Upon our Spirituall Convocation,
And in regard of Causes now in hand,
Which I have open'd to his Grace at large,
As touching France, to give a greater Summe,
[Then] ever at one time the Clergie yet
Did to his Predecessors part withall .

- the danger of the current bill seems to be underscored in the three consecutive non-embellished lines ending F #1, and the phrase opening F #2—suggesting that the Bishop is so appalled that the old 'selfe Bill' is being revised that all of his energies are focused on controlling himself

- certainly the subsequent surround phrase, the only one in the speech, explains his fear ' : if it passe against us/We loose the better halfe of our Possession : ', while the fact that F #2 is slightly more onrushed than modern texts set (which hive off F #2's opening phrase as a separate sentence) again suggests difficulty in maintaining control

- the speech opens carefully enough, (2/1 in the first two lines of F #1, and then the three non-embellished lines discussed above)

- and even if the Bishop's emotions get the better of him in the opening of F #2 (1/3, the first two lines, surround phrase and all), he seems to establish self-control again as he starts to explain that the 'Temporall Lands' (i.e. secular/business property, not land used for religious purposes) will be taken, for intellect returns (4/1, for the next two and a half lines of F #2), at least until the arrival of the (emotional) semicolon

- passion first breaks through as he discusses how many high-rank soldiers the Church is going to be asked to finance (4/3 in the three and a half lines till the next colon), which then becomes emotion when translated into how many people the Church could help with the same money (3/7 plus two extra breath-thoughts—marked ,—in the three lines to the next colon), finishing passionately again with the large sum of money that will be demanded as well (2/1, F #2's last line and a half)

- but the Bishop does manage to regain self-discipline as he suggests that he has a win-win counter-proposal to make (10/1 F #4)

The Life of Henry the Fift
Pistoll

Solus, egregious dog ?
between 2.1.46–80

Background: the following is Pistoll's response to Nym's verbal attacks.

Style: initially one on one, as part of a four handed scene

Where: unspecified, probably a street near the Eastcheap tavern run by the Hostesse

To Whom: Nym, in front of Bardolfe and the Hostesse (Mistris Quickly)

# of Lines: 16

Probable Timing: 0.55 minutes

Take Note: Whereas the F text shows just one section in verse (F #4), suggesting that this is where Pistoll's ire is really roused, most modern texts follow the (non-source text) quarto and set the whole sequence in (very irregular) verse, thus removing the one moment when Pistoll does hit the higher oratorical style. Also, F's orthography shows Pistoll exercising surprising self- control as the speech opens, perhaps suggesting that he is taking care either to avoid a fight or is cautious in case Nym suddenly attacks.

Pistol

1   "Solus," egregious dog ?

2   [O] viper vile !

3   The "solus" in thy most mervailous face,
     The "solus" in thy teeth, and in thy throat,
     And in thy hateful lungs, yea, in thy maw, perdy ;
     And which is worse, within thy nasty mouth !

4   I do retort the "solus" in thy bowels,
     For I can take, and Pistol's cock is up,
     And flashing fire will follow .

5   O [braggart] vile, and damned furious wight,
     The grave doth gape, and doting death is near,
     Therefore exhale .

6   Couple a gorge !

7   That is the word .

8   I [thee defy] again.

9   O hound of [Crete], think'st thou my spouse to get ?

10   No, to the spittle go,
     And from the powd'ring-tub of infamy
     Fetch forth the lazar kite of Cressid's kind,
     Doll Tear sheet she by name, and her espouse .

11   I have, and I will hold, the quondam Quickly
     For the only she; and—pauca, there's enough [ ] !

12   Go to .

Pistoll

1　Solus, egregious dog ?

2　　　　　　　　[ ] Viper vile ; The solus
in thy most mervailous face, the solus in thy teeth, and
in thy throate, and in thy hatefull Lungs, yea in thy Maw
perdy ; and which is worse, within thy nastie mouth .

3　　　　　　　　　　　　　　　　　　　　I
do retort the solus in thy bowels, for I can take, and Pi-
stols cocke is up, and flashing fire will follow .

4　O [Braggard] vile, and damned furious wight,
The Grave doth gape, and doting death is neere,
Therefore exhale .

5　*Couple a gorge*, that is the word .

6　　　　　　　　　　　　　I [defie thee] a-
gaine .

7　O hound of [Creet], think'st thou my spouse to get ?

8　No, to the spittle goe, and from the Poudring tub of in-
　　　　　　　　　　　　　　　　　　　　famy,
fetch forth the Lazar Kite of Cressids kinde, Doll
Teare-sheete, she by name, and her espouse .

9　　　　　　　　　　　　I have, and I will
hold the Quondam Quickely for the onely shee : and
Pauca, there's enough [to] go to .

- thus several of the challenges are very carefully uttered in non-embellished phrases, viz. 'I do retort the solus in thy bowels, for I can take.' plus 'Therefore exhale.' followed by 'think'st thou my spouse to get?' …

- …or in short sentences, the latter showing how close to the edge Pistoll may be, viz. 'Solus, egregious dog?' (F #1) and 'Couple a gorge, that is the word (F #5)—and this spills into the first two surround phrases too

- two of the three surround phrases are emotionally based, not surprisingly both verbal attacks on Nym ' . Viper vile ; ' and throwing his challenge back ' ; and which is worse, within thy nastie mouth . '

- the third is his much more definitive assertion that Mistresse Quickly is in fact his, " : and Pauca, there's enough to go to . "

- thus, after the non-embellished F #1, Pistoll initially moves into somewhat careful passion (5/4 in the eight lines F #2-6)

- but once the subject of Mistresse Quickly comes up, passion breaks through much more unchecked (10/8 in the five and a half lines of F #7-9)

The Life of Henry the Fift
Pistoll

Captaine, I thee beseech to doe me favours :
between 3.6.21–50

Background: it is inevitable that one of the men will be caught red-handed in their thieving. Unfortunately, Bardolfph is the first, and here Pistoll pleads (unsuccessfully) on his behalf.

Style: one on one, as part of a three-handed scene

Where: the English camp

To Whom: Pistoll's captain, Captain Fluellen, in front of Captain Gower

# of Lines: 15

Probable Timing: 0.50 minutes

Take Note: F's orthography shows Pistoll running the full range of release as he appeals to a higher status character for help to save Bardolph—though according to F he never reaches the height of verse as most modern texts that follow the (non-source) quarto suggest.

Pistoll

1   Captain, I thee beseech to do me favors.

2   The Duke of Exeter doth love thee well .

3   Bardolph, a soldier firm and sound of heart,
    And of buxom valor, hath by cruel fate,
    And giddy Fortune's furious fickle wheel,
    That goddess blind,
    That stands upon the rolling restless stone—

4   Fortune is Bardolph's foe, and frowns on him ;
    For he hath stol'n a pax, and hanged must a be—
    A damned death !

5   Let gallows gape for dog, let man go free,
    And let not hemp his windpipe suffocate .

6   But Exeter hath given the doom of death
    For pax of little price .

7   Therefore go speak, the Duke will hear thy voice;
    And let not Bardolph's vital thread be cut
    With edge of penny-cord and vile reproach .

8   Speak, captain, for his life, and I will thee requite .

Pistoll

1 Captaine, I thee beseech to doe me favours : the
Duke of Exeter doth love thee well .

2 Bardolph, a Souldier firme and sound of heart,
and of buxome valour, hath by cruell Fate, and giddie
Fortunes furious fickle Wheele, that Goddesse blind, that
stands upon the rolling restlesse Stone .

3 Fortune is Bardolphs foe, and frownes on him :
for he hath stolne a Pax, and hanged must a be : a damned
death : let Gallowes gape for Dogge, let Man goe free,
and let not Hempe his Wind-pipe suffocate : but Exeter
hath given the doome of death, for Pax of little price .

4 Therefore goe speake, the Duke will heare thy voyce ;
and let not Bardolphs vitall thred bee cut with edge of
Penny-Cord, and vile reproach .

5   Speake Captaine for
his Life, and I will thee requite .

- the surround phrases outline why Pistoll has come to Fluellen,

   ' . Captaine, I thee beseech to doe me favours : ', followed by

   ' . Fortune is Bardolph's foe, and frownes on him : ' which would
   lead to a ' : a damned death: ', so, ' . Therefore goe speake, the
   Duke will heare thy voyce ; '

- when all the excesses are put to one side, the non-embellished lines
  tell the bare bones of Bardolph's doom, and a possible bribe

   'and hang'd must a be: a damned death:' plus 'and vile reproach',
   plus 'and I will thee requite'

- the speech opens highly emotionally (0/3 in the first line), and then
  for the last line of F #1 Pistoll momentarily controls himself (2/0)

- the build-up to the explanation becomes passionate (7/8, F #2)

- the explanation of what has been stolen remains so (2/2, the opening
  line and a half of F #3), then mention of death is non-embellished
  in the next line, and then his outbursts against the 'Gallowes' and
  Exeter's 'doome of death' return as passionate as ever (7/5, the last
  three lines and a bit of F #3)

- the request of F #4-5 is mixed—the first-line initial surround phrase
  appeal for Fluellen to speak to Exeter is emotional (1/4); the end of
  F #4, the hope to avoid hanging is passionate (3/2); the reiteration to
  'Speake' in F #5 is even more so (3/2 in just five words), while the last
  phrase promise of quid pro quo is non-embellished

The Life of Henry the Fift
Constable

The English are embattail'd./To Horse you gallant Princes
4.2.15–37

Background: at last the French call to arms for the battle of Agincourt has been given, and now the Constable issues the command.

Style: general address to a small group

Where: the French camp near Agincourt

To Whom: the Dolphin, the French lords of Orleance, Ramburs, and Beaumont, in front of a Messenger

# of Lines: 24

Probable Timing: 1.15 minutes

Take Note: F's orthography underscores the intellectual and emotional confidence running through the Constable as he prepares his colleagues for the battle to come.

Constable

1   The English are embattled .

2   To horse, you gallant princes! straight to horse !
    Do but behold yond poor and starved band,
    And your fair show shall suck away their souls,
    Leaving them but the shales and husks of men .

3   There is not work enough for all our hands,
    Scarce blood enough in all their sickly veins
    To give each naked curtle-axe a stain,
    That our French gallants shall to-day draw out,
    And sheathe for lack of sport .

4   Let us but blow on them,
    The vapor of our valor will o'erturn them .

5   'Tis positive ['gainst] all exceptions, lords,
    That our superfluous lackeys and our peasants,
    Who in unnecessary action swarm
    About our squares of battle, were enow
    To purge this field of such a hilding foe ;
    Though we upon this mountain's basis by
    Took stand for idle speculation :
    But that our honors must not .

6   What's to say ?

7   A very little little let us doe,
    And all is done .

8   Then let the trumpets sound
    The tucket sonance and the note to mount ;
    For our approach shall so much dare the field,
    That England shall couch down in fear, and yield .

Constable

1　The English are embattail'd,.

2　To Horse you gallant Princes, straight to Horse .

3　Doe but behold yond poore and starved Band,
　And your faire shew shall suck away their Soules,
　Leaving them but the shales and huskes of men .

4　There is not worke enough for all our hands,
　Scarce blood enough in all their sickly Veines,
　To give each naked Curtleax a stayne,
　That our French Gallants shall to day draw out,
　And sheath for lack of sport .

5　　　　　　　　　　　　　　　Let us but blow on them,
　The vapour of our Valour will o're-turne them .

6　'Tis positive [against] all exceptions, Lords,
　That our superfluous Lacquies, and our Pesants,
　Who in unnecessarie action swarme
　About our Squares of Battaile, were enow
　To purge this field of such a hilding Foe ;
　Though we upon this Mountaines Basis by,
　Tooke stand for idle speculation :
　But that our Honours must not .

7　　　　　　　　　　　　　　　What's to say ?

8　A very little little let us doe,
　And all is done : then let the Trumpets sound
　The Tucket Sonnance, and the Note to mount :
　For our approach shall so much dare the field,
　That England shall couch downe in feare, and yeeld .

- the two short opening sentences show how important the intellectu-al opening is to the Constable (4/1, F #1-2)—at last the fight can start

- the derogatory description of the English (the 'poore and starved Band') being too weak to give the French forces enough 'worke' is the only emotionally released passage in the speech (3/8, F #3 and the first two lines of F #4) but finishes with an intellectual anticipa-tion of how easy the battle will be, their unstained weapons sheathed with 'lack of sport' (3/1, the last two and a half lines of F #4)

- the giddy idea of beating them by blowing on them (F #5) is once more emotional (1/4)

- while the idea of the French commoners ('our superfluous Lacquies, and our Pesants') being enough to defeat the English starts out intel-lectually (6/2, the first five lines of F #6), it ends passionately declar-ing their 'Honours' insist they must fight (3/3, the last three lines of F #6)

- thus the short monosyllabic non-embellished F #7 may carry more weight than might at first appear—for, coming where it does, it seems to focus on the inescapable need for honour to be satisfied, rather than the whole event being dismissed as unnecessary

- the surround phrase opening the final sentence sums up the intel-lectual confidence underscoring the French at this stage in the play ' . A very little little let us doe,/And all is done : ', and the speech as a whole—with the final onrushed sentence—provides a passionate encouragement to the field (5/4, F #8)

The Life of Henry the Fift
Pistoll

Doeth fortune play the huswife with me now ?
between 5.1.80–89

Background: though the war is over, it has not been a good time for Pistoll. Not only has Fluellen physically beaten him and forced him to eat a leek, the Welsh national symbol (to pay Pistoll back for the insults he has thrown Fluellen's way), the English captain Gower has called him to task for his behaviour too; but all this pales into insignificance with the news he has received from home.

Style: solo

Where: the English camp

To Whom: direct audience address

# of Lines: 9

Probable Timing: 0.35 minutes

Take Note: As elsewhere, most modern texts set the whole speech in verse. However, F very clearly sets everything in prose until the final startling self-serving and character changing (shaded) vow—which is thus enhanced by being set in heightened verse. By setting everything in verse most modern texts remove this startling theatrical shift.

Pistol

1   Doth Fortune play the huswife with me now ?

2   News have I that my [Nell] is dead i'th spittle
Of a malady of France,
And there my rendezvous is quite cut off .

3   Old I do wax, and from my weary limbs
Honor iscudgell'd.

4   Well, bawd I'll turn,
And something lean to cutpurse of quick hand .

5   To England will I steal, and there I'll steal;
And patches will I get unto these cudgell'd scars,
And [swear] I got them in the Gallia wars.

Pistoll

1   Doeth fortune play the huswife with me now ?

2   Newes have I that my [Doll] is dead i'th Spittle of a mala-
     dy of France, and there my rendevous is quite cut off :
     Old I do waxe, and from my wearie limbes honour is
     Cudgeld .

3   Well, Baud Ile turne, and something leane to
     Cut-purse of quicke hand : To England will I steale, and
     there Ile steale :
     And patches will I get unto these cudgeld scarres,
     And [swore] I got them in the Gallia warres .

- the vehemence of the final verse is enhanced/anticipated by the surround phrase ' : To England will I steale, and there Ile steale : '

- while the speech overall is passionate (10/11), the opening short line sentence (0/1) and final two verse lines (1/2) are more emotional, while the news that his wife is dead is handled intellectually (3/1)

- the most concentrated release is as he reaches the surround phrase conclusion to F #2 ' : Old I do waxe, and from my wearie limbes honour is Cudgeld . ' leading into the opening prose lines of F #3 (6/7)

The Life of King Henry the Eight
Norfolke

Like it your Grace, / The State takes notice of…
between 1.1.100–114 & line 137

Background: after King Henry, undoubtedly the most powerful man in the country is the much loathed and distrusted commoner Cardinal Wolsey, who is both political administrator and church office holder. The Duke of Buckingham is one of the few nobles daring enough to make his opposition to Wolsey public, so much so that he is in danger, as his friend Norfolke now counsels.

Style: as part of a three handed scene

Where: unspecified, presumably a London street

To Whom: the Duke of Buckingham and son-in-law Lord Aburgaveney

# of Lines: 15

Probable Timing: 0.50 minutes

Take Note: Though the sentence structures match, F's orthography, especially the extra breath-thoughts (marked ,) reveal how Norfolke's opening self control cannot be maintained.

Norfolke

1 Like it your Grace,
The state takes notice of the private difference
Betwixt you and the Cardinal .

2   I advise you
(And take it from a heart that wishes towards you
Honor, and plenteous safety) that you read
The Cardinal's malice and his potency
Together ; to consider further, that
What his high hatred would effect wants not
A minister in his power .

3   You know his nature,
That he's revengeful; and I know his sword
Hath a sharp edge ; it's long, and't may be said
It reaches far, and where 'twill not extend,
Thither he darts it .

4   Bosom up my counsel,
You'll find it wholesome .

5   Lo, where comes that rock
That I advice your shunning .

---

6   Say not treasonous .

Norfolke

1   Like it your Grace,
    The State takes notice of the private difference
    Betwixt you, and the Cardinall .

2   I advise you
    (And take it from a heart, that wishes towards you
    Honor, and plenteous safety) that you reade
    The Cardinals Malice, and his Potency
    Together ; To consider further, that
    What his high Hatred would effect, wants not
    A Minister in his Power .

3   You know his Nature,
    That he's Revengefull ; and I know, his Sword
    Hath a sharpe edge : It's long, and't may be saide
    It reaches farre, and where 'twill not extend,
    Thither he darts it .

4   Bosome up my counsell,
    You'l finde it wholesome .

5   Loe, where comes that Rock
    That I advice your shunning .

6   Say not treasonous .

- that he is genuine in his concern for Buckingham can be seen by the non-embellished opening to F #2,

  > "I advise you/(And take it from a heart, that wishes towards you/ Honor, and plenteous safety) "

  and that he regards the danger very seriously can be seen from the surround phrases opening F #3

  > " . You know his Nature,/That he's Revengefull ; and I know, his Sword/Hath a sharpe edge : "

- that the situation is disturbing to him can be seen in the fact that the three sentences completing the speech are all short, and the last doubly weighted by being monosyllabic

- Norfolke starts with seemingly strong mental control (10/2, F #1-2), this, however, seems to be maintained with great difficulty, for four extra breath-thoughts are to be found in this opening section

- then as he talks about Wolsey being 'Revengefull', Norfolke becomes passionate (3/4, F #3), and again emotional as he advises Buckingham to 'Bosome up my counsell' (0/3, F #4)

- but as Wolsey enters, Norfolke moves from passion (1/1, F #5) to great non-embellished care (F #6, 0/0)

The Life of King Henry the Eight
Buckingham

This Butchers Curre is venom'd-mouth'd,
between 1.1.120–158

Background: despite his friend's warning (speech #1 above), Buckingham is still prepared to speak his mind, even after being looked on askance by Wolsey and his cohorts who have just left the stage after crossing before him.

Style: as part of a three handed scene

Where: unspecified, presumably a London street

To Whom: the Duke of Buckingham and son-in-law Lord Aburgaveney

# of Lines: 15

Probable Timing: 0.50 minutes

Take Note: F's orthography reveals a man trying to maintain self-control, but unable to do so, veering between great (enforced?) calm and sudden personal outbursts.

Buckingham

1   This butcher's cur is [venom]-mouth'd, and I
    Have not the power to muzzle him, therefore best
    Not wake him in his slumber .

2   A beggar's book
    Out-worth's a noble's blood .

---

3   I read in's looks
    Matter against me, and his eye revil'd
    Me as his abject object ; at this instant
    He bores me with some trick.

4   He's gone to'th'King ;
    I'll follow and outstare him .

---

5   I'll to the King,
    And from a mouth of honor quite cry down
    This Ipswich fellow's insolence ; or proclaim
    There's difference in no persons .

---

6   {T}his top-proud fellow,

                                I do know
    To be corrupt and treasonous .

---

7   To th'King I'll say't, & make my vouch as strong
    As shore of rock.

Buckingham

1   This Butchers Curre is [venom'd]-mouth'd, and I
     Have not the power to muzzle him, therefore best
     Not wake him in his slumber .

2   A Beggers booke,
     Out-worths a Nobles blood .

3   I read in's looks
     Matter against me, and his eye revil'd
     Me as his abject object, at this instant
     He bores me with some tricke ;He's gone to'th'King :
     Ile follow, and out-stare him .

4   Ile to the King,
     And from a mouth of Honor, quite cry downe
     This Ipswich fellowes insolence ; or proclaime,
     There's difference in no persons .

5   {T}his top-proud fellow,

                      I doe know
     To be corrupt and treasonous .

6   To th'King Ile say't, & make my vouch as strong
     As shore of Rocke :

- the two emotional semicolons, the first establishing the only sur-round phrase in the speech, suggest that despite Norfolke's advice (see speech #1 above), matters are coming to head for Buckingham

  " ; He's gone to the King ; "

  and that in going to the King himself he will deal with Wolsey's 'in-solence ; or proclaime,/There's no difference in persons . '

- nevertheless, from the large number of non-embellished lines in the speech it is evident that Buckingham is taking great care to state his in-flammatory anti-Wolsey opinions with as much self-control as possible

  "I/Have not the power to muzzle him, therefore best/Not wake him in his slumber ."

  "I read in's looks/Matter against me, and his eye revil'd/Me as his abject object,"

  and, since Wolsey has gone to the King,

  "Ile follow, and out-stare him." to plead that "There's difference in no persons." so as to put down "This top-proud fellow,"

- considering that four and a half of F #1-3's seven and a half lines are unembellished, the speech would seem to open as a struggle between mental control and emotion (6/4)

- but envisaging what he'll do once he is with the King leads Buckingham to passion (3/3, F #4)

- despite momentary self-control in referring to Wolsey as the 'top-proud fellow' (the opening of F #5), he shakes of a touch of emo-tion (0/1, the end of F #5), and though mentally alert, he concludes non-rhetorically (F #6, 2/1) with the speech ended by a colon, as if there was more to be said, rather than, as in most modern texts, end-ing with a thought concluding period ending the sentence 'correctly'

The Life of King Henry the Eight
King

Things done well,/And with a care, exempt themselves from feare :
1.2.88–102

Background: despite Wolsey's neatly avoiding the Queene's charge, the King publicly directs Wolsey to rectify the situation nevertheless.

Style: public address, essentially one on one for a larger group to hear

Where: unspecified, but presumably in a public chamber in the palace

To Whom: Cardinal Wolsey, in front of the Queene and those accompanying and siding with her, Norfolke and Suffolke, and those with the King, including Sir Thomas Lovell and unspecified 'Nobles'

# of Lines: 15

Probable Timing: 0.50 minutes

Take Note: As with Wolsey, Henry too has a habit of making his most telling points very quietly, the non-embellished phrases doing all the work for him.

King

1   Things done well
    And with a care, exempt themselves from fear :
    Things done without example, in their issue
    Are to be fear'd .

2   Have you a [precedent]
    Of this commission ?

3   I believe, not any .

4   We must not rend our subjects from our laws,
    And stick them in our will .

5   Sixth part of each ?

6   A trembling contribution !

7   Why, we take
    From every tree, lop, bark, and part o'th'timber ;
    And though we leave it with a root, thus hack'd,
    The air will drink the sap .

8   To every county
    Where this is question'd send our letters, with
    Free pardon to each man that has denied
    The force of this commission .

9   Pray look to't;
    I put it to your care .

King

1   Things done well,
     And with a care, exempt themselves from feare :
     Things done without example, in their issue
     Are to be fear'd .

2   Have you a [President]
     Of this Commission ?

3   I beleeve, not any .

4   We must not rend our Subjects from our Lawes,
     And sticke them in our Will .

5   Sixt part of each ?

6   A trembling Contribution ; why we take
     From every Tree, lop, barke, and part o'th'Timber :
     And though we leave it with a roote thus hackt,
     The Ayre will drinke the Sap .

7   To every County
     Where this is question'd, send our Letters, with
     Free pardon to each man that has deny'de
     The force of this Commission : pray looke too't ;
     I put it to your care .

- thus, though spoken to all as a general maxim, the message that there can be no fear of reprisal provided that

  "Things done well,/And with a care"

  whereas

  "Things done without example, in their issue/Are to be fear'd"

  seems specifically directed towards Wolsey, especially when followed by the amazingly terse short monosyllabic sentence about Wolsey's current taxes

  "Six Part of each?"

- and where the remedy lies is made equally tersely clear in the final phrase

  " : pray looke too't ; /I put it to your care . "

  made all the more important by being monosyllabic and unembellished, heightened even further by being preceded by an emotional surround phrase (created as it is in part with a semicolon)

- despite the apparent ease, it is fairly clear that King Henry is disturbed, for of F's seven sentences, three are short—all as Henry rhetorically questions/ deals with Wolsey directly (F #2, #3 and #5)

- and unlike Wolsey, Henry doesn't seem to control himself intellectually, for overall the speech is passionate (13/10 in fifteen lines), the only truly self-contained moments being F #2, the first direct question of whether Wolsey had any 'President/Of this Commission' (2/0) and the comparative nature image of over-pruning, the first two lines of F #6 (3/1)

The Life of King Henry the Eight
Wolsey

So farewell, to the little good you beare me .
3.2.350–372

Background: despite the order from the King to hand over the Great
Seale (the symbol of power by which he rules), Wolsey remains
stubbornly legally defiant, demanding from his arresting officers
'Where's your Commission?...words cannot carrie/Authority so
weighty'. After much verbal squabbling and accusations, the nobles
exit with the threat 'for your stubborne answer/About the giving
backe the Great Seale to us,/The King shall know it, and (no doubt)
shal thanke you./So fare you well, my little good Lord Cardinall',
which leads to the following.

Style: solo

Where: unspecified, but presumably the palace

To Whom: self and direct audience address

# of Lines: 23

Probable Timing: 1.10 minutes

Take Note: While Wolsey immediately understands what has oc-
curred and the implications of it, the full emotional weight of what
is about to happen doesn't hit till three-quarters of the way through.

Wolsey

1   So farewell—to the little good you bear me .

2   Farewell ? a long farewell to all my greatness!

3   This is the state of man : to-day he puts forth
    The tender leaves of hopes, to-morrow blossoms,
    And bears his blushing honors thick upon him ;
    The third day comes a frost, a killing frost,
    And when he thinks, good easy man, full surely
    His greatness is a ripening, nips his root,
    And then he falls as I do .

4   I have ventur'd,
    Like little wanton boys that swim on bladders,
    This many summers in a sea of glory,
    But far beyond my depth .

5   My high-blown pride
    At length broke under me, and now has left me,
    Weary and old with service, to the mercy
    Of a rude stream, that must for ever hide me .

6   Vain pomp and glory of this world, I hate ye !

7   I feel my heart new open'd .
                                O how wretched

8   Is that poor man, that hangs on princes favors!

9   There is, betwixt that smile we would aspire to,
    That sweet aspect of princes, and their ruin,
    More pangs and fears [than] wars, or women have ;
    And when he falls, he falls like Lucifer,
    Never to hope again .

Wolsey

1   So farewell, to the little good you beare me .

2   Farewell ?

3   A long farewell to all my Greatnesse .

4   This is the state of Man ; to day he puts forth
    The tender Leaves of hopes, to morrow Blossomes,
    And beares his blushing Honors thicke upon him :
    The third day, comes a Frost ;x a killing Frost,
    And when he thinkes, good easie man, full surely
    His Greatnesse is a ripening, nippes his roote,
    And then he fals as I do .

5   I have ventur'd
    Like little wanton Boyes that swim on bladders :
    This many Summers in a Sea of Glory,
    But farre beyond my depth : my high-blowne Pride
    At length broke under me, and now ha's left me
    Weary, and old with Service, to the mercy
    Of a rude streame, that must for ever hide me .

6   Vaine pompe, and glory of this World, I hate ye,
    I feele my heart new open'd .

7   Oh how wretched
    Is that poore man, that hangs on Princes favours ?

8   There is betwixt that smile we would aspire too,
    That sweet Aspect of Princes, and their ruine,
    More pangs, and feares [then] warres, or women have ;
    And when he falles, he falles like Lucifer,
    Never to hope againe .

- the opening shock is made more manifest in F with its three short sentences, as opposed to most modern texts setting them as two, especially since F #1-2 are emotional (0/1) while F #3 leads into a more passionate intellectually led release as he begins to equate man's rise and fall with a frost (6/4, F #3 and the first three and a half lines of F #4)

- but as the image turns to a 'killing Frost' which leads to the inevitable fall, the passion becomes emotionally driven (2/4 in the last three lines)

- even as Wolsey changes the metaphor, comparing himself to a little boy who has swum 'farre beyond my depth', the passion still stays, reverting once more to the slightly intellectual (6/4, F #5)

- but then as he turns to attack 'Vaine pompe, and glory of this World', the emotional dam finally breaks, and his emotions come flooding through (4/11 F #6-8)

- the few surround phrases underscore Wolsey's understanding of his loss, the first two further emphasised by the emotional semicolons

    ' . This is the state of Man ;' leading to ' : The third day, comes a Frost ; '

which then turns to the less emotional, more logical yet still impactful

    " . I have ventur'd/Like little wanton Boyes that swim on bladders : "

finishing with another emotional recognition

    " ; And when he falles, he falles like Lucifer,/Never to hope againe . "

The Life of King Henry the Eight

King

Sir, it doe's not please me,
between 5.2.169–205

Background: the following interrupts an attempted comment by Surrey, another anti-Cranmerite, who gets as far as 'May it please your Grace' before Henry speaks.

Style: general address, initially via one man, for the benefit of all

Where: the Council Chamber

To Whom: Surrey, and thus Gardiner, the Lord Chancellor, Suffolke, Norfolke, and Cromwell

# of Lines: 21

Probable Timing: 1.10 minutes

Take Note: In comparison to the control of his previous speeches, here, when Henry is moved, he does not hold himself back

King

1 　　　　　　　　　　　　{†} Sir, it does not please me .

2 　I had thought I had had men of some understanding
　　And wisdom of my [Council]; but I find none .

3 　Was it discretion, Lords, to let this man,
　　This good man (few of you deserve that title),
　　This honest man, wait like a lousy footboy
　　At chamber-door ? and one as great as you are ?

4 　Why, what a shame was this ?

5 　　　　　　　　　　　　　　Did my commission
　　Bid ye so far forget yourselves ?

6 　　　　　　　　　　　　　　I gave ye
　　Power, as he was a [Councillor] to try him,
　　Not as a groom .

7 　　　　　　　　　There's some of ye, I see,
　　More out of malice [than] integrity,
　　Would try him to the utmost, had ye mean,
　　Which ye shall never have while I live .

8 　{†}　　　　　　　　{M}y Lords respect him,
　　Take him, and use him well ; he's worthy of it .

9 　I will say thus much for him, if a prince
　　May be beholding to a subject, I
　　Am for his love and service so to him .

10 　Once more my Lord of Winchester, I charge you
　　Embrace and love this man .

King

1   {†} Sir, it doe's not please me,
I had thought, I had had men of some understanding,
And wisedome of my [Councell]; but I finde none :
Was it discretion Lords, to let this man,
This good man (few of you deserve that Title)
This honest man, wait like a lowsie Foot-boy
At Chamber dore ? and one, as great as you are ?

2   Why, what a shame was this ?

3   Did my Commission
Bid ye so farre forget your selves ?

4   I gave ye
Power, as he was a [Counsellour] to try him,
Not as a Groome : There's some of ye, I see,
More out of Malice [then] Integrity,
Would trye him to the utmost, had ye meane,
Which ye shall never have while I live .

---

5 {†}   {M}yLords respect him,
Take him, and use him well ; hee's worthy of it .

6   I will say thus much for him, if a Prince
May be beholding to a Subject ;x I
Am for his love and service, so to him .

---

7   Once more my Lord of Winchester, I charge you
Embrace, and love this man .

- that Henry is moved can be seen in the very careful placing of the few extra breath-thoughts (marked ,) scattered through the speech; see especially F #1 where the two thoughts in lines two and three are used to superb effect as Henry tears the flesh off his offending counselors tiny bit by tiny bit

- the onrush of F #1 suggests a Henry who does not wish to control himself in his attack: most modern texts split F #1 into three, and thus make it more carefully precise rather than relentless

- the displeasure he speaks of in opening the speech is not held back emotionally (1/4, the first two and a half lines of F #1), but then Henry recovers self-control, at least for the rest of the sentence, as he describes their appalling behaviour towards Cranmer (4/1)

- but in asking if he had given them permission to treat Cranmer so badly, adding that he sees that some present operate 'More out of Malice than Integrity' and ordering them to treat Cranmer 'well', his passion is aroused (7/6, F #3-5)

- however, in finishing by strongly supporting Cranmer, and once more directly ordering Winchester to do so too, Henry manages to regain self-composure, though the emotional semicolon suggests this is not without difficulty (4/0, F #6-7)

- Henry's underlying emotions can be seen in the fact that all three surround phrases are composed in part by emotional semicolons, as he searches for 'wisdome' in his counselors

    " ; but I finde none : "

or asks for 'respect' and good 'use' for Cranmer, for

    " ; hee's worthy of it . "

to the extent that Henry is fulsome in his own beholding to Cranmer

    " ; I/Am for his love and service, so to him . "

BIBLIOGRAPHY

The most easily accessible general information is to be found under the citations of *Campbell,* and of *Halliday.* The finest summation of matters academic is to be found within the all-encompassing *A Textual Companion,* listed below in the first part of the bibliography under *Wells, Stanley and Taylor, Gary* (eds.)

Individual modem editions consulted are listed below under the separate headings 'The Complete Works in Compendium Format' and 'The Complete Works in Separate Individual Volumes,' from which the modem text audition speeches have been collated and compiled.

All modem act, scene, and/or line numbers refer the reader to *The Riverside Shakespeare,* in my opinion still the best of the complete works, despite the excellent compendiums that have been published since.

The F/Q material is taken from a variety of already published sources, including not only all the texts listed in the 'Photostatted Reproductions in Compendium Format' below, but also earlier individually printed volumes, such as the twentieth century editions published under the collective title *The Facsimiles of Plays from The First Folio of Shakespeare* by Faber & Gwyer, and the nineteenth century editions published on behalf of The New Shakespere Society.

The heading 'Single Volumes of Special Interest' is offered to newcomers to Shakespeare in the hope that the books may add useful knowledge about the background and craft of this most fascinating of theatrical figures.

PHOTOSTATTED REPRODUCTIONS OF THE ORIGINAL TEXTS IN COMPENDIUM FORMAT

Allen, M.J.B. and K. Muir, (eds.). *Shakespeare's Plays in Quarto.* Berkeley: University of California Press, 1981.

Blaney, Peter (ed.). *The Norton Facsimile (The First Folio of Shakespeare).* New York: W.W.Norton & Co., Inc., 1996 (see also Hinman, below).

Brewer D.S. (ed.). *Mr. William Shakespeare's Comedies, Histories & Tragedies, The Second/Third/Fourth Folio Reproduced in Facsimile.* (3 vols.), 1983.

Hinman, Charlton (ed.). *The Norton Facsimile (The First Folio of Shakespeare)*. New York: W.W.Norton & Company, Inc., 1968.

Kokeritz, Helge (ed.). *Mr. William Shakespeare 's Comedies, Histories & Tragedies*. New Haven: Yale University Press, 1954.

Moston, Doug (ed.). *Mr. William Shakespeare's Comedies, Histories, and Tragedies*. New York: Routledge, 1998.

MODERN TYPE VERSION OF THE FIRST FOLIO IN COMPENDIUM FORMAT

Freeman, Neil. (ed.). *The Applause First Folio of Shakespeare in Modern Type*. New York & London: Applause Books, 2001.

MODERN TEXT VERSIONS OF THE COMPLETE WORKS IN COMPENDIUM FORMAT

Craig, H. and D. Bevington (eds.). *The Complete Works of Shakespeare*. Glenview: Scott, Foresman and Company, 1973.

Evans, G.B. (ed.). *The Riverside Shakespeare*. Boston: Houghton Mifflin Company, 1974.

Wells, Stanley and Gary Taylor (eds.). *The Oxford Shakespeare, William Shakespeare , the Complete Works, Original Spelling Edition,* Oxford: The Clarendon Press, 1986.

Wells, Stanley and Gary Taylor (eds.). *The Oxford Shakespeare, William Shakespeare, The Complete Works, Modern Spelling Edition.* Oxford: The Clarendon Press, 1986.

MODERN TEXT VERSIONS OF THE COMPLETE WORKS IN SEPARATE INDIVIDUAL VOLUMES

The Arden Shakespeare. London: Methuen & Co. Ltd., Various dates, editions, and editors .

Folio Texts. Freeman, Neil H. M. (ed.) Applause First Folio Editions, 1997, and following.

The New Cambridge Shakespeare. Cambridge: Cambridge University Press. Various dates, editions, and editors.

New Variorum Editions of Shakespeare. Furness, Horace Howard (original editor.). New York: 1880, Various reprints. All these volumes have been in a state of re-editing and reprinting since they first appeared in 1880. Various dates, editions, and editors.

The Oxford Shakespeare. Wells, Stanley (general editor). Oxford: Oxford University Press, Various dates and editors.

The New Penguin Shakespeare . Harmondsworth, Middlesex: Penguin Books, Various dates and editors.

The Shakespeare Globe Acting Edition. Tucker, Patrick and Holden, Michael. (eds.). London: M.H.Publications, Various dates.

SINGLE VOLUMES OF SPECIAL INTEREST

Baldwin, T.W. *William Shakespeare's Petty School*. 1943.

Baldwin, T.W. *William Shakespeare's Small wtin and Lesse Greeke*. (2 vols.) 1944.

Barton, John. *Playing Shakespeare*. 1984.

Beckerman, Bernard. *Shakespeare at the Globe, I 599-1609*. 1962. Berryman, John. *Berryman 's Shakespeare*. 1999.

Bloom, Harold. *Shakespeare: The Invention of the Human*. 1998. Booth, Stephen (ed.). *Shakespeare's Sonnets*. 1977.

Briggs, Katharine. *An Encyclopedia of Fairies*. 1976.

Campbell, Oscar James, and Edward G. Quinn (eds.). *The Reader's Encyclopedia of Shakespeare*. 1966.

Crystal, David, and Ben Crystal. *Shakespeare's Words: A Glossary & Language Companion*. 2002.

Flatter, Richard. *Shakespeare's Producing Hand*. 1948 (reprint).

Ford, Boris. (ed.). *The Age of Shakespeare*. 1955.

Freeman, Neil H.M. *Shakespeare's First Texts*. 1994.

Greg, W.W. *The Editorial Problem in Shakespeare: A Survey of the Foundations of the Text*. 1954 (3rd. edition).

Gurr, Andrew . *Playgoing in Shakespeare's London*. 1987. Gurr, Andrew. *The Shakespearean Stage, 1574-1642*. 1987. Halliday, F.E. *A Shakespeare Companion*. 1952.

Harbage, Alfred. *Shakespeare's Audience*. 1941.

Harrison, G.B. (ed.). *The Elizabethan Journals*. 1965 (revised, 2 vols.).

Harrison, G.B. (ed.). *A Jacobean Journal*. 1941.

Harrison, G.B. (ed.). *A Second Jacobean Journal*. 1958.

Hinman, Charlton. *The Printing and Proof Reading of the First Folio of Shakespeare*. 1963 (2 vols.).

Joseph, Bertram. *Acting Shakespeare*. 1960.

Joseph, Miriam (Sister). *Shakespeare's Use of The Arts of wnguage*. 1947.

King, T.J. *Casting Shakespeare's Plays*. 1992.

Lee, Sidney and C.T. Onions. *Shakespeare's England : An Account Of The Life And Manners Of His Age*. (2 vols.) 1916.

Linklater, Kristin. *Freeing Shakespeare's Voice.* 1992.

Mahood, M .M. *Shakespeare's Wordplay.* 1957.

O'Connor, Gary. *William Shakespeare: A Popular Life.* 2000.

Ordish, T.F. *Early London Theatres.* 1894. (1971 reprint).

Rodenberg, Patsy. *Speaking Shakespeare.* 2002.

Schoenbaum. S. *William Shakespeare: A Documentary Life.* 1975.

Shapiro, Michael. *Children of the Revels.* 1977.

Simpson, Percy. *Shakespeare's Punctuation.* 1969 (reprint).

Smith, Irwin. *Shakespeare's Blackfriars Playhouse .* 1964.

Southern, Richard. *The Staging of Plays Before Shakespeare.* 1973.

Spevack, M. *A Complete and Systematic Concordance to the Works Of Shakespeare .* 1968-1980 (9vols.).

Tillyard, E.M.W. *The Elizabethan World Picture.* 1942.

Trevelyan, G.M. (ed.). *Illustrated English Social History.* 1942.

Vendler, Helen. *The Art of Shakespeare's Sonnets.* 1999.

Walker, Alice F. *Textual Problems of the First Folio.* 1953.

Walton, J.K. *The Quarto Copy of the First Folio.* 1971.

Warren, Michael. *William Shakespeare, The Parallel King Lear 1608-1623.*

Wells, Stanley and Taylor, Gary (eds.). *Modernising Shakespeare's Spelling, with Three Studies in The Text of Henry V.* 1975.

Wells, Stanley. *Re-Editing Shakespeare for the Modern Reader.* 1984.

Wells, Stanley and Gary Taylor (eds.). *William Shakespeare: A Textual Companion .* 1987.

Wright, George T. *Shakespeare's Metrical Art.* 1988.

HISTORICAL DOCUMENTS

Daniel, Samuel. *The Fowre Bookes of the Civile Warres Between The Howses Of Lancaster and Yorke.* 1595.

Holinshed, Raphael. *Chronicles of England, Scotland and Ireland.* 1587 (2nd. edition).

Halle, Edward. *The Union of the Two Noble and Illustre Famelies of Lancastre And Yorke.* 1548 (2nd. edition).

Henslowe, Philip: Foakes, R.A. and Rickert (eds.). *Henslowe's Diary.* 1961.

Plutarch: North, Sir Thomas (translation of a work in French prepared by Jacques Amyots). *The Lives of The Noble Grecians and Romanes.* 1579.

APPENDIX 1:
GUIDE TO THE EARLY TEXTS

A QUARTO (Q)

A single text, so called because of the book size resulting from a particular method of printing. Eighteen of Shakespeare's plays were published in this format by different publishers at various dates between 1594-1622, prior to the appearance of the 1623 Folio.

THE FIRST FOLIO (F1)'

Thirty-six of Shakespeare's plays (excluding *Pericles* and *Two Noble Kinsmen,* in which he had a hand) appeared in one volume, published in 1623. All books of this size were termed Folios, again because of the sheet size and printing method, hence this volume is referred to as the First Folio. For publishing details see Bibliography, 'Photostated Reproductions of the Original Texts.'

THE SECOND FOLIO (F2)

Scholars suggest that the Second Folio, dated 1632 but perhaps not published until 1640, has little authority, especially since it created hundreds of new problematic readings of its own. Nevertheless more than 800 modern text readings can be attributed to it. The **Third Folio** (1664) and the **Fourth Folio** (1685) have even less authority, and are rarely consulted except in cases of extreme difficulty.

APPENDIX 2:
WORD, WORDS, WORDS

PART ONE: VERBAL CONVENTIONS (AND HOW THEY WILL BE SET IN THE FOLIO TEXT)

"THEN" AND "THAN"

These two words, though their neutral vowels sound different to modern ears, were almost identical to Elizabethan speakers and readers, despite their different meanings. F and Q make little distinction between them, setting them interchangeably . The original setting will be used, and the modern reader should soon get used to substituting one for the other as necessary.

"I," "AY," AND "AYE"

F/Q often print the personal pronoun "I" and the word of agreement "aye" simply as "I." Again, the modern reader should quickly get used to this and make the substitution when necess ary. The reader should also be aware that very occasionally either word could be used and the phrase make perfect sense, even though different meanings would be implied.

"MY SELFE/HIM SELFE/HER SELFE" VERSUS "MYSELF/HIMSELF/HER-SELF"

Generally F/Q separate the two parts of the word, "my selfe" while most modern texts set the single word "myself." The difference is vital, based on Elizabethan philosophy. Elizabethans regarded themselves as composed of two parts, the corporeal "I," and the more spiritual part, the "self." Thus, when an Elizabethan character refers to "my selfe," he or she is often referring to what is to all intents and purposes a separate being, even if that being is a particular part of him- or herself. Thus soliloquies can be thought of as a debate between the "I" and "my selfe," and, in such speeches, even though there may be only one character on-stage, it's as if there were two distinct entities present.

UNUSUAL SPELLING OF REAL NAMES, BOTH OF PEOPLE AND PLACES

Real names, both of people and places, and foreign languages are often reworked for modern understanding. For example, the French town often set in Fl as "Callice" is usually reset as "Calais." F will be set as is.

NON-GRAMMATICAL USES OF VERBS IN BOTH TENSE AND APPLICATION

Modern texts 'correct' the occasional Elizabethan practice of setting a singular noun with plural verb (and vice versa), as well as the infrequent use of the past tense of a verb to describe a current situation. The F reading will be set as is, without annotation.

ALTERNATIVE SETTINGS OF A WORD WHERE DIFFERENT SPELLINGS MAINTAIN THE SAME MEANING

F/Q occasionally set what appears to modern eyes as an archaic spelling of a word for which there is a more common modern alternative, for example "murther" for murder , "burthen" for burden, "moe" for more, "vilde" for vile. Though some modern texts set the Fl (or alternative Q) setting, others modernise. Fl will be set as is with no annotation.

ALTERNATIVE SETTINGS OF A WORD WHERE DIFFERENT SPELLINGS SUGGEST DIFFERENT MEANINGS

Far more complicated is the situation where, while an Elizabethan could substitute one word formation for another and still imply the same thing, to modern eyes the substituted word has an entirely different meaning to the one it has replaced. The following is by no means an exclusive list of the more common dual-spelling, dual-meaning words

anticke-antique	mad-made	sprite-spirit
born-borne	metal-mettle	sun-sonne
hart-heart	mote-moth	travel-travaill
human-humane	pour-(po wre)-power	through-thorough
lest-least	reverent-reverend	troth-truth
lose-loose	right-rite	whether-whither

Some of these doubles offer a metrical problem too, for example "sprite," a one syllable word, versus "spirit." A potential problem occurs in *A Midsummer Nights Dream,* where the modern text s set Q1's "thorough," and thus the scansion pattern of elegant magic can be established, whereas F1's more plebeian "through" sets up a much more awkward and clumsy moment.

The F reading will be set in the Folio Text, as will the modern texts' substitution of a different word formation in the Modern Text. If the modern text substitution has the potential to alter the meaning (and sometimes scansion) of the line, it will be noted accordingly.

PART TWO: WORD FORMATIONS COUNTED AS EQUIVALENTS FOR THE FOLLOWING SPEECHES

Often the spelling differences between the original and modern texts are quite obvious, as with "she"/"shee". And sometimes Folio text passages are so flooded with longer (and sometimes shorter) spellings that, as described in the General Introduction, it would seem that vocally something unusual is taking place as the character speaks.

However, there are some words where the spelling differences are so marginal that they need not be explored any further. The following is by no means an exclusive list of words that in the main will not be taken into account when discussing emotional moments in the various commentaries accompanying the audition speeches.

(modern text spelling shown first)

and- &	murder - murther	tabor - taber
apparent - apparant	mutinous - mutenous	ta'en - tane
briars - briers	naught - nought	then - than
choice - choise	obey - obay	theater - theatre
defense - defence	o'er - o're	uncurrant - uncurrent
debtor - debter	offense - offence	than - then
enchant - inchant	quaint - queint	venomous - venemous
endurance - indurance	reside - recide	virtue - vertue
ere - e'er	Saint - S.	weight - waight
expense - expence	sense - sence	
has - ha's	sepulchre - sepulcher	
heinous - hainous	show - shew	
I'll - Ile	solicitor - soliciter	
increase - encrease	sugar - suger	

APPENDIX 3:
THE PATTERN OF MAGIC, RITUAL &
INCANTATION

THE PATTERNS OF "NORMAL" CONVERSATION

The normal pattern of a regular Shakespearean verse line is akin to five pairs of human heart beats, with ten syllables being arranged in five pairs of beats, each pair alternating a pattern of a weak stress followed by a strong stress. Thus, a normal ten syllable heartbeat line (with the emphasis on the capitalised words) would read as

weak- STRONG, weak - STRONG, weak- STRONG, weak- STRONG, weak- STRONG
(shall I com- PARE thee TO a SUMM- ers DAY)

Breaks would either be in length (under or over ten syllables) or in rhythm (any combinations of stresses other than the five pairs of weak-strong as shown above), or both together.

THE PATTERNS OF MAGIC, RITUAL, AND INCANTATION

Whenever magic is used in the Shakespeare plays the form of the spoken verse changes markedly in two ways . The length is usually reduced from ten to just seven syllables, and the pattern of stresses is completely reversed, as if the heartbeat was being forced either by the circumstances of the scene or by the need of the speaker to completely change direction. Thus in comparison to the normal line shown above, or even the occasional minor break, the more tortured and even dangerous magic or ritual line would read as

STRONG - weak, STRONG- weak, STRONG - weak, STRONG
(WHEN shall WE three MEET a GAINE)

The strain would be even more severely felt in an extended passage, as when the three weyward Sisters begin the potion that will fetch Macbeth to them. Again, the spoken emphasis is on the capitalised words

Pattern of Magic, Ritual & Incantation 189

and the effort of, and/or fixed determination in, speaking can clearly be felt.

> THRICE the BRINDed CAT hath MEW"D
> THRICE and ONCE the HEDGE-Pigge WHIN"D
> HARPier CRIES, 'tis TIME, 'tis TIME.

UNUSUAL ASPECTS OF MAGIC

It's not always easy for the characters to maintain it. And the magic doesn't always come when the character expects it. What is even more interesting is that while the pattern is found a lot in the Comedies, it is usually in much gentler situations, often in songs *(Two Gentlemen of Verona, Merry Wives of Windsor, Much Ado About Nothing, Twelfth Night, The Winters Tale)* and/or simplistic poetry *(Loves Labours Lost* and *As You Like It),* as well as the casket sequence in *The Merchant of Venice.*

It's too easy to dismiss these settings as inferior poetry known as doggerel. But this may be doing the moment and the character a great disservice. The language may be simplistic, but the passion and the magical/ritual intent behind it is wonderfully sincere. It's not just a matter of magic for the sake of magic, as with Pucke and Oberon enchanting mortals and Titania. It's a matter of the human heart's desires too. Orlando, in *As You Like It,* when writing peons of praise to Rosalind suggesting that she is composed of the best parts of the mythical heroines because

> THEREfore HEAVen NATure CHARG"D
> THAT one B0Die SHOULD be FILL'D
> WITH all GRACes WIDE enLARG"D

And what could be better than Autolycus *(The Winters Tale)* using magic in his opening song as an extra enticement to trap the unwary into buying all his peddler's goods, ballads, and trinkets.

To help the reader, most magic/ritual lines will be bolded in the Folio text version of the speeches.

ACKNOWLEDGMENTS

Neil dedicated *The Applause First Folio in Modern Type*
"To All Who Have Gone Before"
and there are so many who have gone before in the sharing of Shakespeare through publication. Back to John Heminge and Henry Condell who published *Mr. William Shakespeares Comedies, Histories, & Tragedies* which we now know as The First Folio and so preserved 18 plays of Shakespeare which might otherwise have been lost. As they wrote in their note "To the great Variety of Readers.":

> Reade him, therefore; and againe, and againe : And if then you doe not like him, surely you are in some manifest danger, not to understand him. And so we leave you to other of his Friends, whom if you need, can be your guides: if you neede them not, you can lead yourselves, and others, and such readers we wish him.

I want to thank John Cerullo for believing in these books and helping to spread Neil's vision. I want to thank Rachel Reiss for her invaluable advice and assistance. I want to thank my wife, Maren and my family for giving me support, but above all I want to thank Julie Stockton, Neil's widow, who was able to retrive Neil's files from his old non-internet connected Mac, without which these books would not be possible. Thank you Julie.

Shakespeare for Everyone!

Paul Sugarman, April 2021

AUTHOR BIOS

Neil Freeman (1941-2015) trained as an actor at the Bristol Old Vic Theatre School. In the world of professional Shakespeare he acted in fourteen of the plays, directed twenty-four, and coached them all many times over.

His groundbreaking work in using the first printings of the Shakespeare texts in performance, on the rehearsal floor and in the classroom led to lectures at the Shakespeare Association of America and workshops at both the ATHE and VASTA, and grants/fellowships from the National Endowment for the Arts (USA), The Social Science and Humanities Research Council (Canada), and York University in Toronto. He prepared and annotated the thirty-six individual Applause First Folio editions of Shakespeare's plays and the complete *The Applause First Folio of Shakespeare in Modern Type*. For Applause he also compiled *Once More Unto the Speech, Dear Friends*, three volumes (Comedy, History and Tragedy) of Shakespeare speeches with commentary and insights to inform audition preparation.

He was Professor Emeritus in the Department of Theatre, Film and Creative Writing at the University of British Columbia, and dramaturg with The Savage God project, both in Vancouver, Canada. He also taught regularly at the National Theatre School of Canada, Concordia University, Brigham Young University.. He had a Founder's Ring (and the position of Master Teacher) with Shakespeare & Company in Lenox, Mass: he was associated with the Will Geer Theatre in Los Angeles; Bard on the Beach in Vancouver; Repercussion Theatre in Montreal; and worked with the Stratford Festival, Canada, and Shakespeare Santa Cruz.

Paul Sugarman is an actor, editor, writer, and teacher of Shakespeare. He is founder of the Instant Shakespeare Company, which has presented annual readings of all of Shakespeare's plays in New York City for over twenty years. For Applause Theatre & Cinema Books, he edited John Russell Brown's publication of *Shakescenes: Shakespeare for Two* and The Applause Shakespeare Library, as well as Neil Freeman's Applause First Folio Editions and *The Applause First Folio of Shakespeare in Modern Type*. He has published pocket editions of all of Shakespeare's plays using the original settings of the First Folio in modern type for Puck Press. Sugarman studied with Kristin Linklater and Tina Packer at Shakespeare & Company where he met Neil Freeman.

www.ingramcontent.com/pod-product-compliance
Lightning Source LLC
Chambersburg PA
CBHW070330090426
42733CB00012B/2425